# JUST LISTEN TO THIS

To Marda
With best wishes
Elizabeth Urch
Oct. 25 @ 1997

# Just Listen To This

### Through the Year with
## Elizabeth Urch

*[signature: Elizabeth Urch]*

ARTHUR JAMES

BERKHAMSTED

First published in 1997 by

ARTHUR JAMES LTD
70 Cross Oak Road
Berkhamsted
Hertfordshire HP4 3HZ

A catalogue record for this book is available
from the British Library.

ISBN 0 85305 370 7

Typeset in Baskerville by Watermark
Cromer NR27 9HL

Printed in Great Britain by
The Ipswich Book Company

It is the province of knowledge to speak
and it is the privilege of wisdom to listen.
*Oliver Wendell Holmes*

This book is dedicated to all those whose lives, one way or another, have been interwoven with mine. It has been my privilege to listen to them and to gain much from what they have said. Their forbearance when they were obliged to listen to me instead, whether they wished to or not, was always commendable.

# FOREWORD

Our youngest child, 20-year-old Marie, died in an IRA bomb explosion on Remembrance Day in Enniskillen, November 8th 1987. We were plunged into shock, grief and despair. Elizabeth Urch reached out to us in sympathy and understanding by sending us a most touching letter and a signed copy of her book *Be Still My Soul*. In the January following my dear daughter's death I was very sad, depressed and distressed. I began reading *Be Still My Soul* and I was gripped by the contents of the book. It stilled my soul when I realised how God had guided and brought Elizabeth through thorny paths and through loss and great grief. The book contains the very powerful sermon which her husband preached on 1 Peter 4:12, a verse God had brought to my notice some days after Marie died. Walter Urch's sermon explained the whole meaning of this profound verse. The entire book became a balm to my aching heart, and each member of my family was greatly helped by reading *Be Still My Soul*.

I have come to know the author, Elizabeth Urch, and to cherish her warm and sincere friendship. I appreciate her deep spiritual insight and her humorous common touch. It was with great joy and anticipation that I learnt she was compiling *Just Listen To This*. The completed book contains a gem for every day of the year and the insets for Easter and Christmas prepare our minds and concentrate our thoughts for those great Christian festivals each year. Each month has its own lovely seasonal introduction. There is great variety in the book. I enjoyed the travel tales from many countries. She has included many stories written in her own unique style. There is a store of beautiful Bible passages, poetry, proverbs, humorous tales and Elizabeth's own well-expressed prayers. She has also included some very beautiful and deep, soul-searching prayers written by Michael, her son, who is a Lutheran minister in Finland.

There is a wealth of material in this book for the reader. It is my privilege to commend *Just Listen To This*. In reading, listening and absorbing its contents, lives will be enriched, renewed and drawn closer to the Master.

*Joan Wilson, Enniskillen*

7

# JANUARY

*For what has been – Thanks!*
*To what shall be – Yes!*

*Dag Hammarskjold*

**January 1st**
Here is a blessing for any child born this year. Adapt it as you
need to, changing 'him' to 'her' if necessary, and inserting the
child's name after the first line:

IRISH BLESSING FOR A CHILD

We wish to the new child . . .
A heart that can be beguiled
   By a flower,
   That the wind lifts
   As it passes
Over the grasses
After a summer shower

A heart that can recognise
Without aid of the eyes
   The gifts that life holds
   For the wise.

When the storms break for him
May the trees shake for him
   Their blossoms down.

In the night that he is troubled
May a friend wake for him
   That his time be doubled.

And at the end of all loving and love
   May the Man Above
   Give him a crown.

**January 2nd**
I used to live beside a wonderful old man, who on his ninetieth
birthday told me his five-year plan for his garden. He lived long
enough to see well over half of his optimistic project completed.

9

## January 3rd

My youngest grandchild, when aged three, was walking with his mother in the Åland Islands which lie between Helsinki and Stockholm. There's plenty of water around that archipelago, but not much in the way of a river. Very excited when he came on a restless little stream, he asked his mother, 'Where is it going?'

'To the sea,' she answered.

A fairly long silence ensued, and then with all the profundity of a three-year-old he continued, 'How does it know where the sea is?'

At the start of this new year we may feel like that restless stream, not quite sure where the journey will take us. We need not travel alone. St Augustine once said of God, 'You have made us for yourself, and our hearts are restless until we find rest in you.'

## January 4th

I wonder have you heard of Archy, the cockroach who was companion to Don Marquis, an American writer. Maybe you're not finding a lot to be thankful for at the start of this new year's journey. But Archy said there was always something to be thankful for. You would imagine there wasn't much a cockroach could be thankful about. But Archy said when the fishing season started, he grew very cheerful at the thought that nobody had ever come up with the idea of using cockroaches for bait.

## January 5th

When God has told you what you ought to do, he has already told you what you can do. *Joan of Arc*

## January 6th

And what of ourselves? With all these witnesses to faith around us like a cloud, we must throw off every encumbrance, every sin to which we cling, and run with resolution the race for which we are entered, our eyes fixed on Jesus, on whom faith depends from start to finish. *Hebrews 12:1–2 (NEB)*

## January 7th

This prayer I call my fortress prayer. It is a good one with which to start the new year:

> Circle us, Lord
> Keep protection near and danger afar
> Circle us, Lord
> Keep hope within and doubt without
> Circle us, Lord
> Keep light near and darkness afar
> Circle us, Lord
> Keep peace within, and evil out.

## January 8th

Just before the war in Yugoslavia commenced, I was walking high in the Macedonian mountains there. A shepherd gave me his hand-whittled staff to help me over a rough track and then told me to keep it. Sadly, because of a last-minute rush to the airport, I left it on a bus. I wrote to the company, hoping to have it returned. It never turned up, but instead I had a hand-written note of apology in quaint English from the Yugoslavian who had done the search for the staff. He signed it, 'With sorrow, from your friendly Lost and Found Officer.'

I am sure that every good quality displayed in human nature must be found in ever greater abundance in God's nature. A Macedonian shepherd helped me negotiate a rough path; a Dubrovnik bus employee offered a friendly word. How much more will God!

## January 9th

A youngster I know was being chided for sucking his thumb.

'My mouth happens to need my thumb just now,' he retorted.

I didn't ask if he'd just been told to put a stopper in it.

## January 10th

Tony's use of his thumb reminds me of how shaking someone's hand in greeting came to be the custom. It was because if a man was shaking your hand he would be quite unable to get at his sword to strike you a treacherous blow. The only time I ever visited Switzerland, we had two accidents in one day. One was a collision between two cars, and the other between a train and a tractor at a level crossing. No one was injured, and I was interested to see that on each occasion the main participants shook hands before getting to grips with the discussion about blame and damage. Today when we hear so much about 'road rage', that would seem a good policy to adopt.

## January 11th

> A word is dead
> When it is said,
> Some say.
> I say it just
> Begins to live
> That day.
>
> *Emily Dickinson*

## January 12th

Someone said of a travel writer that he was very hard to get to know, because although he was always with people, his travels ensured that he was always with different people. And that is a kind of solitariness, where you are not required to give too much of your inner self.

## January 13th

Is there a man among you who will offer his son a stone when he asks for bread, or a snake when he asks for fish? If you, then, bad as you are, know how to give your children what is good for them, how much more will your Heavenly Father give good things to those who ask him!

Always treat others as you would like them to treat you: that is the Law and the prophets.　　　*Matthew 7:9-12 (NEB)*

## January 14th

Dear Lord, just as others have served us with cheerfulness and gladness, help us so to serve you. Bless those who find the road they are travelling rough, perhaps with sorrow or some kind of loss at the end of it. Give us not only an assurance of human kindness, but the knowledge that you yourself are waiting there for us.

**January 15th**

ALL I EVER REALLY NEEDED TO KNOW
I LEARNT IN KINDERGARTEN

Most of what I really need to know about how to live, and what
to do, and how to be, I learnt in Kindergarten. Wisdom was not
at the top of the graduate school mountain, but there in the
sandbox at nursery school.

These are the things I learnt. Share everything. Play fair.
Don't hit people. Put things back where you found them. Clean
up your own mess. Don't take things that aren't yours. Say
you're sorry when you hurt somebody. Wash your hands
before you eat. Flush. Warm cookies and cold milk are good
for you. Live a balanced life. Learn some and think some and
draw and paint and sing and dance and play and work every
day some. Take a nap every afternoon. When you go out into
the world, watch for traffic, hold hands and stick together. Be
aware of wonder. Remember the little seed in the plastic cup.
The roots go down and the plant goes up, but nobody really
knows how or why, but we are all like that.

Goldfish and hamsters and white mice and even the little
seed in the plastic cup – they all die. So do we.

And then remember the book about Dick and Jane and the
first word you learnt, the biggest word of all: LOOK. Everything you need to know is in there somewhere. The Golden
Rule and basic sanitation. Ecology and politics and sane living.
Think of what a better world it would be if we all – the whole
world – had cookies and milk about three o'clock every afternoon and then lay down with our blankets for a nap. Or if we
had a basic policy in our nation and other nations to always put
things back where we found them and cleaned up our own
messes. And it is still true, no matter how old you are, when you
go out into the world, it is best to hold hands and stick together.

*Robert Fulghum, Seattle*

**January 16th**

All the knowledge I possess everyone else can acquire. But my
heart is all my own.                                    *Goethe*

**January 17th**

One little girl I knew told me one day that she had the cleverest Granny in the whole world. When I enquired about what she could do that the rest of us couldn't, she floored me by saying, 'She is able to take her teeth out at night and put them in a glass of water.'

**January 18th**

People are nostalgic for goodness. *Desmond Tutu*

**January 19th**

CHILDREN LEARN WHAT THEY LIVE

If a child lives with criticism
He learns to condemn.

If a child lives with hostility
He learns to fight.

If a child lives with ridicule
He learns to be shy.

If a child lives with shame
He learns to feel guilty.

If a child lives with tolerance
He learns to be patient.

If a child lives with encouragement
He learns to be confident.

If a child lives with praise
He learns to appreciate.

If a child lives with fairness
He learns about justice.

If a child lives with security
He learns about faith.

If a child lives with approval
He learns to like himself.

If a child lives with acceptance
He learns to give love to the world.

*Author unknown*

**January 20th**

At that time the disciples came to Jesus and asked, 'Who is the greatest in the kingdom of Heaven?' He called a child, set him in front of them, and said, 'I tell you this: unless you turn around and become like children, you will never enter the kingdom of Heaven. Let a man humble himself till he is like this child, and he will be the greatest in the kingdom of Heaven. Whoever receives one such child in my name receives me.'                                        *Matthew 18:1–5 (NEB)*

**January 21st**

> O God, make us children of quietness
> And heirs of peace.                    *Clement of Rome*

**January 22nd**

Some years back, when I was at the Hardanger Fiord in Norway, I met a ninety-year-old who was very frail physically, but very animated as she related to me what her childhood had been like in that beautiful area. She knew no English and I knew no Norwegian, but her son translated for me. When I was leaving – never to meet her again – I asked her son to give her a message from me. I said I wanted her to know that I had done many interesting things in Norway, but none more interesting than meeting her. After Anders, her son, had put this into Norwegian for her, I heard her answer with a very sharp retort, followed by gales of laughter from her family. What she had said was, 'People always find antiques interesting.'

**January 23rd**

> As a white candle in a holy place
> So is the beauty of an aged face
> As the spent radiance of the winter sun
> So is a woman with her travail done
> Her brood gone from her and her thoughts as still
> As the waters under a ruined mill.        *Joseph Campbell*

## January 24th

Put up in a place where it's easy to see
The cryptic admonishment T T T.
When you feel how depressingly slowly you climb
It's well to remember that Things Take Time.

*Unattributed*

## January 25th

Young pupil writing about his family: 'My Granny's face has lines like my corduroy trousers, but she says she still feels young inside of her face.'

## January 26th

There's a divinity that shapes our ends,
Rough-hew them how we will.

*Shakespeare:* **Hamlet**

## January 27th

And behold, there was a man in Jerusalem, whose name was Simeon; and the same man was just and devout, waiting for the consolation of Israel: and the Holy Ghost was upon him. And it was revealed unto him by the Holy Ghost, that he should not see death, before he had seen the Lord's Christ. And he came by the Spirit into the temple: and when the parents brought in the child Jesus, to do for him after the custom of the law, then took he him up in his arms, and blessed God and said, Lord, now lettest thou thy servant depart in peace, according to thy word: for mine eyes have seen thy salvation, which thou hast prepared before the face of all people; a light to lighten the Gentiles, and the glory of thy people Israel. *Luke 2:25–32 (AV)*

## January 28th

Dear Lord, you know every one of us, young and old, who are on this pilgrimage of life together. Help us to listen to each other and to your Holy Spirit so that we can bring our own offering of understanding and desire for light and peace in your world.

**January 29th**

Some talk of millimetres and some of kilogrammes
And some of decilitres, to measure beer and drams,
But I'm a British workman, too old to go to school
So by pounds I'll eat, and by quarts I'll drink
And I'll work by my three-foot rule.

You might imagine that recent developments have caused this defiant little verse. It was in fact written by Rankine, one of Britain's great engineers, in 1864.

**January 30th**

I read
In a book
That a man called Christ
Went about doing good.
It is very disconcerting
To me
That I am so easily satisfied
With just
Going about.                    *Unattributed*

**January 31st**

So here we are at the end of the first month of the year, and some of you might be saying 'the bitter end'. That saying took on a new meaning for me recently when I discovered that it probably originated from a nautical term. It was used by the sailors when the boat was anchored and 'the bitter end' was the part of the cable attached to the 'bitts' in the stern of the ship. I hope you feel your anchorage is safe and sure as you review this first month of the year's journey.

A journey of a thousand miles begins with a single step.
                    *An old Chinese saying*

# FEBRUARY

*If Winter come, can Spring be far behind?*

*Shelley*

### February 1st

A SIXTEENTH-CENTURY LETTER

I salute you:

There is nothing I can give you which you have not got: but there is much, very much, that while I cannot give it, you can take.

No heaven can come to us unless our hearts find rest in today. Take heaven!

No peace lies in the future which is not hidden in this present little instant. Take peace!

The gloom of the world is but a shadow. Behind it, yet within our reach, is joy.

There is radiance and glory in the darkness, could we but see, and to see, we only have to look.

I beseech you to look.

And so at this time I greet you. Not quite as the world sends greetings, but with profound esteem and with prayer that for you now and for ever the day breaks and the shadows flee away.                                                                 *Fragiovanni*

### February 2nd

> Joy is peace dancing.
> Peace is joy at rest.

### February 3rd

Sign outside a church in St Helen's, Merseyside:

Carpenter from Nazareth requires joiners. Apply within.

### February 4th

An old dominie (head teacher) in Scotland got very impatient with his class.

'I tellt ye! I tellt ye!' he complained.

A schools inspector of my acquaintance said, 'That man was a good teacher. He took the trouble to tell them twice.'

## February 5th

An eighteenth-century Eton schoolboy wrote a letter home about this time of the year:

I wright to tell you I am very retched and my chilblains is worse again. I have not made any progress and I do not think I shall. I am sorry to be such an expense to you, but I do not think this schule is very good. There are black beetles in the kitchen and sometimes they cook them in the dinner which can't be very holesome when you're not strong. Dear Mama, I hope you and Papa are well and don't mind me being uncomfortable because I don't think I'll last very long. Please send me some more money as I owe one of the boys 8 pennies. . . .

## February 6th

You must live at peace among yourselves. And we would urge you to admonish the careless, encourage the faint-hearted, support the weak, and to be very patient with them all.

See to it that no one pays back wrong for wrong, but always aim at doing the best you can for each other and for all people.

Be always joyful; pray continually; give thanks whatever happens; for this is what God in Christ wills for you.

*1 Thessalonians 5:14–18 (NEB, adapted)*

## February 7th

O Jesus, Master Carpenter of Nazareth, who on the cross with wood and nails hast wrought man's full salvation, wield well thy tools in this thy workshop, that we who come to thee rough-hewn may be fashioned to a truer beauty by thy hand. Amen.

*Author unknown*

## February 8th

A MODERN BUILDING PROJECT

The Lord said unto Noah, 'Where is the ark I commanded you to build?' and Noah answered, 'Verily I have three carpenters off sick. The gopher wood supplier hath let me down – yea, even though the gopher wood hath been on order for nigh upon twelve months. The damp course specialist hath not turned up.'

And God said to Noah, 'I want the Ark finished before seven days and seven nights.'

Noah said, 'It will be so.' But it was not so.

The Lord said to Noah, 'What seemeth to be the trouble this time?'

Noah said, 'My sub-contractor hath gone bankrupt. The pitch for the outside of the ark hath not arrived. The glazier departeth on holiday to Majorca, yea, even though I offered him double time. Shem hath formed a pop group with his brethren Ham and Japheth. Lord, I am undone.'

The Lord grew angry and said, 'What about the animals? Two of every sort I have ordered to be kept alive. Where for example are the giraffes?'

And Noah said, 'They have been delivered to the wrong address, but should arrive by Friday.'

And the Lord said to Noah, 'Where are the monkeys, and the elephants and the zebras?'

Noah said, 'They are expected today.'

The Lord said, 'How about the unicorns?'

Noah wrung his hands and wept. 'Oh Lord, Lord, they are a discontinued line. Thou canst not get unicorns for love nor money. Thou knowest, thou knowest how it is.'

And the Lord said, 'Noah, my son, I know. Why else dost thou think I sent a flood?'                                   *Unattributed*

### February 9th
Another wise saying by Archy the cockroach:

The bees got their governmental system settled millions of years ago. But the human race is still groping.

### February 10th
One sceptic has said that Mysticism starts with a mist, centres on I and ends with a schism.

**February 11th**

One of our eminent politicians said that efficiency means doing immediately what can be done immediately.

And one of his colleagues said of him that he had the finest mind of anyone he had ever met, except when it was made up.

**February 12th**

> Go to a tree in silence. You will find
> In the soft eloquence of bud and leaf
> Security beyond the voice of grief
> And faith beyond the reach of humankind.
>
> Men spend their noisy days in search of gain
> While trees find God in sunlight, soil and rain.

*Author unknown*

**February 13th**

Do not store up for yourselves treasure on earth, where it grows rusty and moth-eaten, and thieves break in to steal it. Store up treasure in heaven, where there is no moth and no rust to spoil it, no thieves to break in and steal. For where your treasure is, there will your heart be also.

*Matthew 6:19–21 (NEB)*

**February 14th**

Lord God, in the confusion of our times we so often get our priorities wrong. Help us to seek the light which will reveal to us the corners of our being which we hide even from ourselves.

**February 15th**

A few years back I had some Norwegians staying with me and as my neighbours had interesting tales to tell, I went round one morning and said, 'It would be fun if we could all have supper together tonight. What about it?' Delighted! So the time was set for 7.30.

That hour came and went and fifteen minutes later, when my sandwiches were showing signs of curling up for the night, I went out to look down the road to see if my neighbours were on their way. There was no one in sight, so I went back to tell my Norwegians that north of Dunkeld, punctuality is not necessarily considered a virtue. After another fifteen minutes,

I emerged again, without success. At 8.15 I finally decided something must be amiss, and set off rather apprehensive to my neighbours' house.

'Come in! Come in!' they cried with relief. 'The supper is not yet spoiled! But where are your friends?'

We were even more highly amused when we realised that we had been emerging at different times to look up and down the road – just like the weather puppets we had as children to give us a forecast of rain or fine. So it is that the same words can mean different things to different people. Very light-hearted on that occasion, but sadly, not always so. Before we indulge in recriminations, it's good to pause and think what may have caused a misunderstanding. Someone needs to take the initiative to clear it up. Maybe it should be me!

## February 16th

> He that lets the small things bind him
> Leaves the great undone behind him.

## February 17th

After Alec Douglas-Home had addressed a Tory gathering in a village hall near where I live, the chairwoman's enthusiasm was so great that she addressed the party faithful with the words, 'Now, friends, after all that Sir Alec has said, I urge you to go out from here, and vote as you've never voted before!'

## February 18th

> The road to wisdom?
> Well, it's plain
> And simple to express:
> To err and err and err again
> But less and less and less.          *Unattributed*

## February 19th

It is only with the heart that one can see rightly: what is essential is invisible to the eye.

*From* The Little Prince *by Antoine de Saint-Exupéry*

**February 20th**

There are some odd mistranslations in various versions of the Bible. An old Bible called the She Bible is in Dunkeld Cathedral, near where I live. Apparently one of the first authorised versions in 1611 reads in Ruth 3:15: 'And *he* went into the town.' The second reads: 'And *she* went into the town.' Most of the modern versions use that, though I am told that the original Hebrew is *he*. The Hebrew writer could have made a mistake – he could hardly blame it on his typewriter or wordprocessor!

A more serious mistranslation is from the Greek in John 10:16. Two separate Greek words have been translated as 'fold' whereas the second one, I am told, should correctly be translated as 'flock'. This makes a big difference to the interpretation of the verse, which becomes: 'Other sheep I have which are not of this fold: them also I must bring, and they shall hear my voice. And there shall be one flock and one shepherd.' As Professor William Barclay elucidates it, 'A flock can be distributed amongst many different folds and still belong to the one owner.' A great help, this, as we try to keep ecumenism alive and well.

**February 21st**

> O Lord, thou knowest how busy I must be this day:
> If I forget thee, do not thou forget me.
>
> *Prayer before the Battle of Edgehill*
> *by Sir Jacob Astley (1579–1652)*

**February 22nd**

I used to think I was poor. . . . Then they told me I wasn't poor. I was needy. . . . Then they told me it was self-defeating to think of myself as needy. I was deprived. . . . Then they told me deprived was a bad image, I was underprivileged. . . . Then they told me underprivileged was overused. I was disadvantaged.

I still don't have a dime – but I have a great vocabulary.

> *Jules Feiffer*

**February 23rd**

Overheard in a school staffroom:
'This class knows damn all.'
'Good! If they can spell it, start from there.'

**February 24th**
Recently I lost a dear friend, called Heather, who for years had been crippled with multiple sclerosis. She could talk most profoundly about deep matters, but you would always leave her with laughter in your heart, for she had a pawky sense of humour. Before she went for her last stay in hospital she had a couple of hens which ran in and out of her little cottage.

I asked her, 'Do you get an egg for your tea every day?'

Quick as a shot, she replied, 'Well I don't know what religion these hens are, but I never seem to get one on a Friday.'

**February 25th**
When I was in Karelia in Finland I saw a picture of a fish with some Finnish writing under it. I asked for it to be translated and it was this prayer which I had already known for a long time. My Finnish friend had bought it for her husband whose fishing exploits in Lapland were always being related to her.

FISHERMAN'S PRAYER

Lord, suffer me to catch a fish
So large that even I
In talking of it afterwards
Shall have no need to lie.

**February 26th**
Son, returning home from school with his report:

'I'm afraid this report is not very good, Dad. Do you think it's heredity or environment?'

**February 27th**
When the Lord turned again the captivity of Zion, we were like them that dream. Then was our mouth filled with laughter, and our tongue with singing: then said they among the heathen, The LORD hath done great things for them. The LORD hath done great things for us; whereof we are glad.

*Psalm 126:1–3 (AV)*

## February 28th

Lord God, thank you for joy, pleasure, merriment and laughter. For those whose lives are so hard and bitter that they feel they will never smile again, we especially pray. Be to them a strong consolation and please turn again the tide of their misfortunes.

## February 29th (for a Leap Year)

By the nature of things every year should be 365¼ days, so to keep the balance we have this extra day every four years – easily remembered as the last two digits of the date are exactly divisible by 4. It is called Leap Year because the fixed festivals such as Christmas and New Year's Day, which normally come one day later in the week than they did the previous year, all leap over a day of the week following February 29th. I have never found out why it became acceptable for the woman to make the proposal of marriage in a Leap Year, but there was actually a law passed in Scotland in 1288 to say that in every year known as Leap Year a maiden lady had the liberty to 'bespeak the man she liked' and if he refused to take her, he must pay her a pound. You could soon run up a fortune if you were wily enough, for a pound was a lot of money in the thirteenth century. A similar law was passed in France and it became legal custom also in Genoa and Florence 200 years later. I begin to wonder if these laws were ever repealed – and, if so, why?

# MARCH

**March 1st**

### A CELTIC BLESSING

May the blessing of light
Be on you, light without and light within.

May the blessed sunlight
Shine upon you and warm your heart till it glows
Like a great peat fire, so the stranger may
Come and warm himself at it, and also a friend.

And may the light shine out of the eyes of you
Like a candle set in the windows of a house
Bidding the wanderer to come in out of the storm.

And may the blessing of the rain
Be on you – the soft sweet rain. May it fall upon
Your spirit so that the little flowers may spring up
And shed their sweetness on the air.

And may the blessing of the great rains be on you
May they beat upon your spirit and wash it fair and clean
And leave there many a shining pool where the blue
Of Heaven shines, and sometimes a star.

And may the blessing of the earth
Be on you – the great round earth;
May you ever have a friendly greeting
For them that pass as you're going along the roads.

May the earth be soft under you when
You rest upon it, tired at the end of the day.
And may it rest easy over you when
At the last, you lie out under it.
May it rest so lightly over you that

Your soul may be up and off from under it quickly
And up and off on its way to God.
And now may the Lord bless you and bless you kindly.

## March 2nd
If you bake bread with indifference, you bake a bitter bread
that feeds but half man's hunger.                    *Kahlil Gibran*

## March 3rd
> Twinkle, twinkle little star,
> I don't wonder what you are.
> You're the cooling down of gases,
> Forming into solid masses.                    *Unattributed*

## March 4th
I was eavesdropping one day when my daughter was giving her
own little daughter a bit of a roasting for asking someone for
sweets that had been sitting on a hostess's table.
  'Wait until you are offered one in future!'
  'Well, sometimes people forget to offer you one.'
  'Just wait until they remember.'
  A few minutes later my grand-daughter arrived in the
kitchen where I had been eavesdropping.
  'Granny, if I don't ask you for an ice-cream after I've had my
lunch, will you remember to give me one?'

## March 5th
> Losing one glove is certainly painful
> But nothing compared to the pain
> Of losing one,
> Throwing away the other
> Then finding the first one again.                    *Unattributed*

## March 6th
> Better a pittance with the fear of the LORD
> than great treasure and trouble in its train.
> Better a dish of vegetables if love go with it
> than a fat ox eaten in hatred.
> Bad temper provokes a quarrel,
> but patience heals discords.
>
>                    *Proverbs 15:16–18 (NEB)*

## March 7th

MORNING PRAYER

Now another day is breaking
Sleep was sweet and so was waking
Dear Lord, I promised you last night
Never again to sulk or fight
Such vows are easier to keep
When a child is fast asleep
Today, O Lord, for your dear sake
I'll try to keep them when awake.

*From* Parents Keep Out *by Ogden Nash*

## March 8th

Of all the mementoes I have of a visit I paid to Australia some years back, perhaps the strangest are four old Australian pennies. They were given to me by a couple I met briefly. They had been victims of the great Ash Wednesday bush fires which had raged in 1983. These folk had lost all their cattle and a new bungalow home into which they were just about to move. The furniture had been installed on Shrove Tuesday, and they hadn't completed the insurance so it was a total loss. The irony was that to get to the new bungalow, the fire had leapt right over the old shack that they were vacating, leaving it totally unharmed. All they found in the ashes of their new home were some old Australian pennies and they gave me a few. Those coins remind me of the couple's cheerful disposition in the face of their loss – and of the determined manner in which they set about adding on rooms to the old shack. They said they were thankful to have each other and a base to get going again.

## March 9th

I used to complain about having no shoes to put on, until I met a man who had no feet. *Old Chinese saying*

## March 10th

For the first time we had a woman minister appointed to the village church. My young class were writing letters to imaginary friends in a foreign country describing our school and the folk in it. One nine-year-old who had just learnt about using a PS finished off with: 'I forgot to tell you that we now get a weekly visit from the new village priestess.'

## March 11th

ON A MODERN PHILOSOPHER

Atheist once, he now with knowing nod
Proclaims himself on nodding terms with God.

*G. J. Blundell*

## March 12th

A parish priest at an International Rugby Match in Dublin:
'Heel the ball, man, to the glory of God.'
And why not?

## March 13th

The Lord is near; have no anxiety, but in everything make your requests known to God in prayer and petition with thanksgiving. Then the peace of God, which is beyond our utmost understanding, will keep guard over your hearts and your thoughts, in Christ Jesus. *Philippians 4:6–7 (NEB)*

## March 14th

God grant me the serenity
to accept the things I cannot change,
the courage to change the things I can
and the wisdom to know the difference.

*Reinhold Niebuhr*

## March 15th

A young lad writing about St Patrick said, 'When St Patrick was a wee boy, he wasn't a saint at all.' That reminded me of a time many years ago when it was a regular thing to see a group of ministers in the city square where I lived, talking to a crowd about religion. A slightly inebriated man walked by, shouting, 'Sure, Jesus was only a working man.' I wondered if he thought that the ministers with their collars turned round the wrong way were not working men. Or maybe like the child writing about St Patrick, had he a desire to find a point of humanity with a saint, or even a Saviour?

## March 16th

I do not like my state of mind
I'm bitter, querulous, unkind;
I hate my legs, I hate my hands,
I do not yearn for lovelier lands.

I dread the dawn's recurrent light
I hate to go to bed at night
I snoot at simple earnest folk
I cannot take the gentlest joke.

I find no peace in paint or type
My world is but a lot of tripe.
I'm disillusioned, empty-breasted,
For what I think, I'd be arrested.

I am not sick, I am not well,
My quondam dreams are shot to hell.
My soul is crushed, my spirit sore,
I do not like ME any more.        *Unattributed*

## March 17th

St Patrick wasn't an Irishman, but was born around 389 in a place called Bannavem, which was either in Wales or Scotland. He first went to Ireland as a slave and tended sheep on Slemish, a mountain near where I was born. He escaped to Gaul and then had a supernatural call to return to Ireland to teach them about Christianity. He used the three-leaved shamrock to demonstrate the Trinity, the Three in One. There are many legends about him, chiefly that he cleared Ireland of its snakes, the last defiant one being enticed into a box before being cast into the sea. Pliny, an early writer whose encyclo-paedic works were used for about a thousand years, had written long before Patrick's time that serpents refused to go anywhere near shamrock, so perhaps that is how Patrick earned his repu-tation for banishing snakes.

## March 18th

I was once near the well of St Bridget in the West of Ireland. When I was in the Post Office in the village nearby, I asked who St Bridget was.

'Sure, I wouldn't know,' was the reply. 'She was long before my time.'

I have since learnt that she lived about the time of St Patrick and founded Ireland's first monastery which admitted both men and women. She was their abbess and she wrote a very practical little prayer:

'O God, please bless my kitchen, that there may always be enough in it to give to those in need.'

## March 19th

Are you a practising Catholic?'

'No. I'm a submarine Catholic. I only surface when I'm in trouble.'

## March 20th

### THE TRINITY

Though God has never been seen by any man, God himself dwells in us if we love one another; his love is brought to perfection within us.

Here is the proof that we dwell in him and he dwells in us: he has imparted his Spirit to us. Moreover, we have seen for ourselves, and we attest, that the Father sent the Son to be the saviour of the world.             *1 John 4:12–14 (NEB)*

## March 21st

### ST PATRICK'S BREASTPLATE

Christ be with me, Christ within me,
Christ behind me, Christ before me,
Christ beside me, Christ to win me,
Christ to comfort and restore me,
Christ beneath me, Christ above me,
Christ in quiet, Christ in danger,
Christ in hearts of all that love me,
Christ in mouth of friend and stranger.

## March 22nd

During the world cup in South Africa in June 1995, Thandi, a Zulu woman, was interviewed about the Boks, as she called them. (They had springboks decorating their rugger shorts.) There was only one non-white in the team. Yet listen to what Thandi had to say:

'I have no idea what they are doing or why. I can't see why

they spend all that time sitting on each other, or making themselves into that tortoise thing. All I know is I'm glued to the screen and when I see the team in green hugging each other I get damp in my eyes. Those are my team. Those are my boys.'

We can all get damp in the eyes when we hear that sort of proclamation, recognising that the years of bitterness are gradually being washed away.

**March 23rd**

>         Fanatics
>         may defend
>             a point of view
>         so strongly
>         as to prove
>             it can't be true.          *Unattributed*

**March 24th**

'Comparative religion is an admirable recipe for making people comparatively religious.'          *Mgr Ronald Knox*

**March 25th**

It's many a year since I wrote down this comment on legislative verbosity, made by Sir Alex Alexander, who was Chairman of the British Food Export Council at the time. I dread to think how the figures have snow-balled since then:

The Lord's Prayer contains 56 words. The Ten Commandments 297 words. The American Declaration of Independence 300 words. The Common Market Regulation on the import of caramel contains 26,911 words.

**March 26th**

>     If of thy mortal goods thou are bereft
>     And from thy tender store two loaves alone are left,
>     Sell one, and with the dole
>     Buy hyacinths to feed thy soul.
>             *Sadi, Persian poet of the twelfth century*

**March 27th**

What doth the LORD require of thee, but to do justly, and to love mercy, and to walk humbly with thy God?          *Micah 6:8 (AV)*

**March 28th**

> Lord, make me an instrument of your peace.
> Where there is hatred, let me sow love;
> Where there is injury, pardon;
> Where there is discord, union;
> Where there is doubt, faith;
> Where there is despair, hope;
> Where there is darkness, light;
> Where there is sadness, joy.  *St Francis of Assisi*

**March 29th**

I do not seek to understand in order to believe. I believe in order that I might understand.

*St Anselm of Canterbury (1038–1109)*

**March 30th**

Now that winter is behind us and spring ahead with all the pains and pleasures facing us in the garden I will give you for the last two days of the month some words about the out-of-doors:

> A grasshopper sat on a flagstone and wept
> With sorrow that few surpass.
> He had painfully mastered his letters and leapt
> To a place where he knew an inscription was kept
> And of course it was KEEP OFF THE GRASS.

*Unattributed*

**March 31st**

> I am a humble artist
> Moulding my earthly clod,
> Adding my labour to Nature's,
> Simply assisting God.
>
> Not that my effort is needed;
> Yet, somehow I understand
> My Maker has willed it that I should have
> Unmoulded clay in my hand.

*Unattributed*

# 'NO STORY SO DIVINE'
## *Meditations as we approach Easter*

### Approaching Easter (1)

One year I was about to read in Mark 12 about Jesus in the Temple when the widow with her two tiny coins came in. At about the same time I read this cautionary tale which I believe originated with the early Communists. Afterwards I read the biblical tale with new insight into what true sacrifice meant as Jesus saw it.

'If you had two houses, what would you do?'
'Keep one and give one to the state.'
'If you had two cars what would you do?'
'Keep one and give one to the state.'
'If you had two chickens what would you do?'
'Keep them both.'
'Why?'
'Well, you see I just happen to have two chickens.'

I suddenly realised the enormity of the woman's gift. We should have thought her quite generous if she had kept one coin, and had given one to the Temple. That would still have been sacrificial, using our human and materialistic standards. But here, 2,000 years later, we still remember her, for Jesus said she, with less than enough, gave *all* that she had. I'm sure this humble widow herself would not have comprehended the full importance of her gift which today is recorded amongst all the historic happenings of that crucial time in God's plan of complete sacrifice from his Son. It is significant that earlier in the same chapter of Mark we hear Jesus saying that there is only one God and that we must love him with all our heart, soul and mind and with all our strength.

It is a significant and salutary tale to remember, as we sing and pray again this Eastertide:

> Were the whole realm of nature mine
> That were an offering far too small
> Love so amazing, so divine
> Demands my soul, my life, my all.

## Approaching Easter (2)

Another woman who seemed to be wantonly extravagant in her giving we read of in Matthew 26. Divine extravagance! She had used a costly ointment to anoint Jesus – it could even have been worth as much as a year's wages for a workman. But maybe the material cost is not so great as the cost she had to pay in facing up to the carping criticism of those who were also disciples. The words of Jesus are very strange as he himself was preparing for death. 'She did it for my burial.'

Sydney Carter captures the emotion of the moment:

> Said Judas to Mary, 'Now what will you do
> With your ointment so rich and so rare?'
> 'I'll pour it all over the feet of my Lord
> And I'll wipe it away with my hair,' she said,
> 'I'll wipe it away with my hair.'

> 'Oh Mary, oh Mary, just think of the poor:
> This ointment it could have been sold,
> And think of the blankets and think of the bread
> You could buy with the silver and gold,' he said,
> 'You could buy with the silver and gold.'

> 'Tomorrow, tomorrow, I'll think of the poor;
> Tomorrow,' she said, 'Not today,
> For dearer than all of the poor of the world
> Is my Love who is going away,' she said,
> 'Is my Love who is going away.'

> Said Jesus to Mary, 'Your love is so deep,
> Today you may do as you will,
> Tomorrow you say I am going away
> But my body I leave with you still,' he said,
> 'My body I leave with you still.

> 'The poor of the world are my body,' he said,
> 'To the end of the world they shall be;
> The bread and the blankets you give to the poor
> You'll find you have given to me,' he said,
> 'You'll find you have given to me.

> 'My body will hang on the cross of the world
> Tomorrow,' he said, 'and today,
> And Martha and Mary will find me again

And wash all my sorrows away,' he said,
'And wash all my sorrows away.'

## Approaching Easter (3)

The story of Christ in Gethsemane, the Olive Garden, as told in
Matthew 26 is one of forsakenness after his washing of the disciples' feet, and after his transformation of the Passover Feast
into the Lord's Supper or the Eucharist as we now call it. Luke
in his recording uses unfathomable words about the
Gethsemane scene that can be translated as 'they (the disciples)
were sleeping for sorrow'. I am sure that when Christ asked
that God should remove his cup of sorrow, it did not have so
much to do with the physical suffering. Grievous as that was,
the mental and spiritual suffering and the sense of alienation
and of loneliness as revealed in 'My God, My God, why have
you forsaken me?' show suffering of a different and more cruel
dimension.

But it was in Gethsemane that his battle was won.

> Into the woods my Master went,
> Clean forspent, forspent.
> Into the woods my Master came,
> Forspent with love and shame.
> But the olives were not blind to him,
> The little grey leaves were kind to him:
> The thorn-trees had a mind to him
>     When into the woods he came.
>
> Out of the woods my Master went,
> And he was well content.
> Out of the woods my Master came,
> Content with death and shame.
> When death and shame would woo him last,
> From under the trees they drew him last:
> 'Twas on a tree they slew him – last
>     When out of the woods he came.          *Sidney Lanier*

## Approaching Easter (4)

I went to a commemoration service in a Memorial garden on
the fiftieth anniversary of VJ Day. I wanted especially to think
of an Australian friend, Roma Page, the widow of Dr Bob Page
who had been beheaded by the Japanese. His story was told in

Robert Mackie's *The Heroes*, which documented the events leading up to the deaths of Bob and his colleagues.

As the silence of commemoration was called for, suddenly I had an extra hurt, for casual passers-by were pushing their way through the gathered crowd, licking their ice-creams and drinking their cans of Coke. I was shocked by their nonchalance.

As I pondered this I suddenly thought that it must also have been so in parts of Jerusalem on the day that Jesus was taken out to die. Crucifixion was a common form of execution then, and a passer-by without any emotion may just have said, 'Oh, they're all gathered because of another three crucifixions today.' W. R. Rodgers' poem came to mind:

> 'And when they had scourged Jesus
> he delivered him to be crucified.'

They took him out to die
The lark was shaking out its acres of song in the sky
And the sun shone. People looked up and remarked
What a wonderful day it was going to be
And the cheery boys ran on in front of the crowd
And the cheeky ones wanted to stare.

Once he noticed
A blind man whom he had healed looking at him
With horrified eyes as if to say
'Was it for this I was given my sight by God that day?'
He turned away. If only this had been an important death
If only he knew the people who barracked him now
Had been travelling years and years to reach this place
But they were casual passers-by and their interest was jaded.

Yet it was all as he had expected, and
He would not avoid or evade it. Far away
A spool of birds was spinning above the hill,
And still Pilate sat in the empty court beneath
Sucking seeds of thoughtfulness through his teeth.

*W. R. Rodgers*

Is it nothing to you, all ye that pass by? behold, and see if there be any sorrow like unto my sorrow.     *Lamentations 1:12 (AV)*

**Approaching Easter (5)**

We have thought of those present on the day of execution who were possibly nonchalant. It is helpful to find out to whom the last words on the cross were addressed. Christ did not say anything individual to those who were ignoring him, castigating him or gambling over his robe – or to the unrepentant thief. His words were about them, rather than to them. He spoke to God, asking that they might be forgiven (Luke 23). There is a moment which touches me deeply, showing how he shared our human needs (John 19), where he said, 'I thirst'. This reminds me of the human side of his life. When amongst us, he needed rest and sleep; he needed food and drink; he needed companionship as well as solitude. Here I find again Emmanuel – God with us.

The words to the repentant thief are not only words of forgiveness, but also reassurance of reunion.

The last words of our loved ones are very precious to us. So I am sure both Mary, Christ's mother, and John would treasure always those words when Jesus committed Mary to John's care. I think they would talk often in John's home about that, and remember also the agony of his own feeling of separation from his Father in heaven when he cried out, 'Why have you forsaken me?' And then the more triumphant words, 'It is finished', followed by the committal of his soul to the Father he so recently felt had forsaken him.

As we stand again at the Cross, in contemplation of the Passion of our Lord, we can be assured that Christ will have a word for us, and each one of us individually.

> Our sins, not thine, thou bearest, Lord;
> Make us thy sorrow feel
> Till through our pity and our shame
> Love answers Love's appeal.
>
> Grant us to suffer with thee, Lord,
> That as we share this hour
> Thy cross may bring us to thy joy
> And resurrection power.
>
> *Peter Abelard*

## Approaching Easter (6)

As we wait for Easter Day, let us think of Christ's sacrifice in these words written by Theodulf of Orleans in the eighth century:

'Wherefore the scars of Christ's passion remained in
the body of his resurrection.'

When Christ came from the shadows by the stream of
    Phlegethon
Scars were upon his feet, his hands, his side.
Not, as dull souls might deem,
That he, who had the power
Of healing all the wounds whereof men died,
Could not have healed his own,
But that those scars had some divinity
  Carriage of mystery,
Life's source to bear the stigmata of Death.

By these same scars his men
Beheld the very body that they knew,
  No transient breath
  No drift of bodiless air,
And held him in their hearts in fortress there.
They knew their Master, risen and unfurled,
The hope of resurrection through the world.

By these same scars, in prayer for all mankind,
  Before his Father's face,
He pleads our wounds within his mortal flesh,
And all the travail of his mortal days,
Forever interceding for his grace,
Remembering where forgetfulness were blind,
Forever pitiful, forever kind,
Instant that Godhead should take thought for man,
Remembering the manhood of his Son,
His only Son and the deep wounds he bore.
By those same scars, his folk will not give o'er
Office of worship, whilst they see
  Passion, thy mystery:
In those dark wounds their weal,
In that descent to Hell, their climb to the stars,
  His death, their life,
  Their wreath, his crown of thorns.

## Easter Day

I only once had the opportunity to spend Easter Day in an Eastern Orthodox church, and my chief memory of the joyous occasion was the wondrous shout which reverberated round the church. 'Christ is risen!' was proclaimed by the priest and loudly and triumphantly answered by the congregation, 'He is risen indeed!' If anyone today were to give me the opportunity to introduce one new thing to *all* our churches here I should request, 'Please, could our service on Easter Day always start with that triumphant statement of belief?' Even outside the church in Greece people were greeting each other joyfully with these words, and I felt I was experiencing some of the joy that must have been felt on that very first Easter Day. The whole fabric of Christianity is woven around this central theme of Christ's resurrection. It wasn't just that he had survived death – he had defeated it.

I cannot attempt to explain the Resurrection, but I must proclaim it. My belief is that at any time God wishes, he can break into this world he has created to reveal himself to us. It is all mystery, and meant I believe to remain so until the time when we see Christ face to face. Meantime we can experience for ourselves the Risen Lord.

Christ's followers did not immediately recognise him. Mary mistook him for the gardener – until he called her by her name. That is a very moving thing to me, for we recognise so well the tone of voice used when someone who loves us calls us by name.

The disciples on the shore of Galilee mistook him for a stranger and recognised him only after he helped them with their job of catching fish. The two disciples on the road to Emmaus only recognised him when he broke bread in a familiar way.

Christ still comes to those who are searchers after his truth. It is no surprise to me that the risen Christ often reveals himself to those who for one reason or another must endure suffering, because he was raised through his own suffering. If at first we do not recognise his presence, in our own dark hours of doubt and sorrow and questioning, that does not mean that he is absent from us. When we allow him to find us, and allow him to call us by our name, we will then be able to say with Julian of Norwich, 'Though not yet, all will again be well, and all will finally be well.' That is the confidence given to us when we accept that Christ is alive.

# CHRIST IS RISEN! ALLELUIA!

## ON EASTER DAY

When Mary thro' the garden went,
  Her eyes, for weeping long, were dim,
The grass beneath her footsteps bent,
  The solemn lilies, white and slim,
  These also stood and wept for him.

When Mary thro' the garden went,
  She sought, within the garden ground,
One for whom her heart was rent,
  One who for her sake was bound,
  One who sought and she was found.

*Mary Coleridge*

Love ever lives
Forgives
Outlives
Ever stands with open hands
And while it lives,
It gives
For this is Love's prerogative
To give
And give
And give.

*Author unknown*

# APRIL

*April, April, laugh thy girlish laughter*
*Then the moment after*
*Weep thy girlish tears.*            *Sir William Watson*

## April 1st

I was walking in the Lake District some years back when I came
on an old Quaker Meeting House which had within it a copy of
Desiderata which follows. The credit was given to an Episcopa-
lian Church in Baltimore where they said the piece had originated in 1692. I found that information was wrong as the
words had been written by Max Ehrmann, a Terre Haute,
Indiana, poet in 1927. The words were wrongly attributed due
to the fact that a priest of the church, liking the piece, printed it
for his congregation on Church paper which had on it the date
the church was built in 1692. So it is that people can be fooled,
or careless, even about such important things.

### ADVICE FOR LIVING
### DESIDERATA

Go placidly amid the noise and the haste, and remember what
peace there may be in silence. As far as possible, without surrender, be on good terms with all persons. Speak your truth
quietly and clearly and listen to others, even the dull and ignorant: they too have their story. Avoid loud and aggressive persons; they are vexatious to the spirit. If you compare yourselves
with others you may become vain and bitter; for always there
will be greater and lesser persons than yourself. Enjoy your
achievements as well as your plans. Keep interested in your
own career, however humble; it is a real possession in the
changing fortunes of time. Exercise caution in your business
affairs, for the world is full of trickery. But let not this blind
you to what virtue there is. Many persons strive for high ideals,
and everywhere life is full of heroism. Be yourself. Especially
do not feign affection. Neither be cynical about love, for in the
face of all aridity and disenchantment, it is as perennial as the
grass. Take kindly the counsel of the years, gracefully surren-
dering the things of youth. Nurture strength of spirit to shield

you in sudden misfortune. But do not distress yourself with imaginings. Many fears are born of fatigue and loneliness. Beyond a wholesome discipline, be gentle with yourself. You are a child of the universe no less than the trees and the stars; you have a right to be here. And whether or not it is clear to you, no doubt the universe is unfolding as it should. Therefore be at peace with God, whatever you conceive Him to be. And whatever your labours and aspirations, in the noisy confusion of life, keep peace with your soul. With all its sham, drudgery and broken dreams, it is still a beautiful world. Be cheerful. Strive to be happy.

## April 2nd

> The mind which planned the march of suns
>> Can understand
> The petty trials of my day:
>> And surely He
>> Who hollowed out the cup which holds
>> The mighty sea
>> And keeps the waves in check, can give
>>> Tranquillity.                    *Unattributed*

## April 3rd

One day I was shopping in a supermarket when I saw a little episode which happens all too frequently, when children see laid out all the goodies which are far more tempting than the sensible foods their parents are intent on purchasing. The little four-year-old boy was demanding some ghastly sickly sticky sweets which his mother refused to buy. At first he wheedled and coaxed, then tried the usual blackmail of humiliating his mother as she waited in a long queue, by howling at the top of his voice. When she ignored him, his final weapon was to shout at her, 'I hate you! I hate you! I hate you!' We were embarrassed for her as we waited for her retort, and then we realised that we were in the presence of a saint. She gently ruffled his hair and said, 'Well, if that's true, then it's a good job that I have enough love for the two of us.' She had probably never had a lesson in psychology in her life, but she had the priceless gift of wisdom and commonsense, as well as a big heart.

**April 4th**

> As eternity is reckoned
> There is a lifetime in a second.

**April 5th**

AN EPITAPH

> So walked she from her birth
> In simpleness and gentleness
> And honour and clean mirth.

**April 6th**

> A soft answer turns away anger,
> but a sharp word makes tempers hot.
> A wise man's tongue spreads knowledge;
> stupid men talk nonsense.
> The eyes of the LORD are everywhere,
> surveying evil and good men alike.
> A soothing word is a staff of life,
> but a mischievous tongue breaks the spirit.
>
> *Proverbs 15:1–4 (NEB)*

**April 7th**

The prayer today is taken from the wall plaques in Coventry Cathedral:

> In industry –
> God be in my hands and in my making
> In education –
> God be in my mind and in my growing
> In the home –
> God be in my heart and in my loving
> In government –
> God be in my plans and in my deciding
> In the arts –
> God be in my senses and in my creating.

**April 8th**

A few years back around springtime, I decided to indulge in one of those unambitious nostalgic pleasures which delight us as we get older. I wanted to go again to Durham and to the banks of the River Wear underneath the Cathedral where

45

Cuthbert and the Venerable Bede had walked. I had never been there since the later years of World War 2 when I had a brief reunion with the man who was eventually to become my husband. We faced a long separation before our marriage. So it is natural that I can remember our words to each other. I had no difficulty finding the spot near Prebends Bridge, and my mind was filled with sadness as I thought of how brief our life had been together, for death took him as a young man still at the peak of his powers. I wished we could have shared that nostalgic moment together. But I had absolutely no notion of the joy that was to follow my sad thoughts. I walked a short distance from the bridge and almost passed by a copse of dead elm trees which had been destroyed by Dutch Elm disease. I did not realise until I was close that I could enter the small grove, there to find the most exquisite carvings entitled THE UPPER ROOM, representing the Last Supper. Every bowl, every dish, every vine leaf had been lovingly carved by a young local sculptor called Colin Wilbourn. I was chastened and fortified as I went back again and again to study his work. He had used one of Nature's disasters to make a thing of beauty. My husband had been like a mature, strong tree stripped bare by an intemperate disease. Our tragedy could also be changed by spiritual creativity into a thing of beauty.

### April 9th

All which I took from thee I did but take,
    Not for thy harms,
But just that thou might'st seek it in My arms.
    All which thy child's mistake
Fancies as lost, I have stored for thee at home:
    Rise, clasp My hand, and come!
        *Francis Thompson: 'The Hound of Heaven'*

### April 10th

There is no means to annul
One gesture, one word.
These are all tissue of time, these are all
Immortal. . . .
So this is the sum of it, this
Say not it is not much
You cannot unkiss that kiss
You cannot untouch that touch.    *Francis Meynell*

**April 11th**
There are ways of losing that are conquest. There are ways of gaining that are loss.

**April 12th**
Fynn, in his extraordinary book *Mister God, This is Anna*, says that after the immediate grief of Anna's death when he finally made some sense out of everything and found some peace, he spoke to God in the way Anna would have spoken, by telling him, 'Good old Mister God. You might be a bit slow at times, but you certainly make it all right in the end.'

**April 13th**
Beloved, think it not strange concerning the fiery trial which is to try you, as though some strange thing happened unto you: but rejoice, inasmuch as ye are partakers of Christ's sufferings; that, when his glory shall be revealed, you may be glad also with exceeding joy. . . . Wherefore let them that suffer according to the will of God commit the keeping of their souls to him in well doing, as unto a faithful Creator.     *1 Peter 4:12–13, 19 (AV)*

**April 14th**
Lord God, when disaster and disappointment strike, help us to seek that moment of recognition, that insight that will carry us forward beyond our grief. Show us how to embrace a situation we cannot change. Thank you for the deeper and richer knowledge you can impart to us through it. You know we want that knowledge, but you also know that in our human ignorance we would prefer to gain it in some less painful way. Deliver us from perplexity of mind and thought on this matter. Inspire us by your Spirit to make something positive and even beautiful out of our disasters.

**April 15th**

THIS SIDE OF CALVIN

The Rev. Mr Harcourt, folk agree
Nodding their heads in solid satisfaction,
Is just the man for this community:
Tall, young, urbane, but capable of action.
He pleases where he serves. He marshals out
The younger crowd, lacks trace of clerical unction,

Cheers the Kwanis and the Eagle Scout,
Is popular at every public function,

And in the pulpit elegantly speaks
On divers matters both with wit and clarity –
Art, education, God, the early Greeks,
Psychiatry, St Paul, true Christian charity,
Vestry repairs that surely must begin –
All things but Sin. He seldom mentions Sin.

I don't know who wrote that, but imagine it was an American. It set me thinking, and I was fascinated to find out that the records of Christ's dealings with people who needed healing far out-numbered the records of his direct dealings with those *described* as sinners. Most of the latter are recorded in Luke, which I find particularly intriguing since Luke was a doctor. That doesn't mean of course that Christ was ever far away from the presence of sinners, for we all fall into that category. He was with them always, and with compassion, as he remains with us too.

### April 16th

The devil is fairly voted out
And of course the devil's gone
But simple folks would like to know
Who carries his business on.

### April 17th

When I was living in Northern Ireland in the sixties, there was a Manse family living some miles away with a young son who, despite their best efforts, caused them constant despair by his irreligious vocabulary. After being severely rebuked yet again one day, he decided to leave home. He studiously packed his little lunch box whilst surreptitiously searching the apparently unconcerned faces of his parents. They watched as he wandered around the Manse glebe and the orchard, after he'd slammed the door behind him. Later, as dusk was falling, and having eaten all his food, he sheepishly returned and rang the doorbell.

'So you've decided to return home?' said his Dad.

'Well, where the hell did you think I could go?' was his retort.

## April 18th

One of my youngsters did a similar thing to that other Manse nipper, when she told me emphatically one day, after some cross words, that I could take her back to where I'd bought her. I said, 'Well, that's a journey to the hospital then, so you'll need to get your coat on.'

She was evidently determined to depart glamorously, for she went off and dressed herself in her Sunday best. As she was very tiny, I suggested that perhaps she would need help in coping with the traffic, so she agreed that I should see her safely on her way. We hadn't walked more than a few yards, when she put out her arms and asked to be taken home. Not much more was said at that point, but when I was bathing her that evening, she wound her bare little body around mine, sobbing, and pleaded, 'If I ever do say anything like that again, Mummy, will you make sure you don't believe me?'

I promised her that, and with the tears dried, she then said, 'If I had gone to the hospital, would they have given you back all you paid for me?'

## April 19th

The trouble with some sin is that it can be far too pleasurable, as St Augustine realised all too well. He wrote in his *Confessions* in the fifth century that he had prayed: 'Lord, give me chastity and continence – but do not give it to me just yet.' Some fourteen centuries later, Chalib, a Turkish poet, also realised the same lure when he prayed: 'O Lord, it is not the sins that I have committed that I regret. It is those that I have had no opportunity to commit.'

And as Igor Stravinsky said nearer to our own time, 'Sins cannot be undone, only forgiven.'

## 20th

> Happy the man whose disobedience is forgiven,
>     whose sin is put away!
> Happy is a man when the LORD lays no guilt to his account,
>     and in his spirit there is no deceit.      *Psalm 32:1–2 (NEB)*

Blessed are they whose iniquities are forgiven, and whose sins are covered. Blessed is the man to whom the Lord will not impute sin.      *Romans 4:7–8 (AV)*

## April 21st

Jehovah – Father, Spirit, Son –
Mysterious Godhead, Three in One,
Before your throne we sinners bend.
Grace, pardon, life to us extend.

## April 22nd

Alfred, Lord Tennyson, had an uncle called Charles, who when he heard that his nephew had made a book of poems, said, 'I wish he could have made something more useful like a wheelbarrow.' Strange how we arrive at the value of different kinds of work. Strange, too, how the monetary rewards for different kinds of work can be so diverse. All our hackles rise when we hear that someone has a monthly increase in salary greater than an honest worker's entire yearly income. We balk at the inequalities, especially if we happen to be at the lower end of the scale. Even here we most readily reserve our animosities for those who have just gone up the ladder of reward a little higher than ourselves. It has been recorded that Rockefeller's chauffeur had very little resentment against Rockefeller for his many millions. What really incensed him was when he realised how much more the local cab-driver earned compared to himself.

## April 23rd

Don Marquis's companion Archy, the cockroach, had a very philosophical way of regarding the layers of importance in the human race. He said that insects had their own point of view regarding civilisation. A man thinks he amounts to a great deal, but to a flea or a mosquito a human being was merely something good to eat.

## April 24th

I had the task of putting my youngest grandchild, then aged nearly 3, to bed. After numerous bedtime stories finally I said time was up and he must get to sleep. He said he couldn't possibly as he had a lot of work to do. When I enquired further, he announced that he still hadn't written his sermon! He comes from a line of ministers!

**April 25th**

> My Bishop's eyes I've never seen
> Though light in them may shine
> For when he prays, he closes his
> And when he preaches – mine! *Author unknown*

**April 26th**

And what is it to work with love?
It is to weave the cloth with threads drawn from your heart, even as if your beloved were to wear that cloth.
It is to sow seeds with tenderness and reap the harvest with joy, even as if your beloved were to eat the fruit.
It is to charge all things you fashion with a breath of your own spirit. . . .
Work is Love made visible. *Kahlil Gibran*

**April 27th**

The gifts we possess differ as they are allotted to us by God's grace, and must be exercised accordingly: the gift of inspired utterance, for example, in proportion to a man's faith; the gift of administration, in administration. A teacher should employ his gift in teaching, and one who has the gift of stirring speech should use it to stir his hearers. If you give to charity, give with all your heart; if you are a leader, exert yourself to lead; if you are helping others in distress, do it cheerfully.

Love in all sincerity, loathing evil and clinging to the good. Let love for our brotherhood breed warmth of mutual affection. Give pride of place to one another in esteem.

With unflagging energy, in ardour of spirit, serve the Lord.
*Romans 12:6–11 (NEB)*

**April 28th**

O God, you are the searcher of all our hearts. In our work and amongst our colleagues we have adopted cloaks and disguises, but before you there is nothing hidden. You know whether we put in an honest day's toil for the money we will be paid. You know whether we have worked humbly and with self-denial. For some it is harder than for others. There is the man who takes no joy in the type of work he is doing, but he holds on to it for the security it offers his dependants. There are employers who find their employees truculent and uncooperative, and there are employees who find their employers harsh and unfeeling. Give us one and all a sense of each other's needs.

As we hope for peaceful sleep at night, bless those who are just becoming involved in important and dedicated night work. Be with the nurse, the doctor and the relative, as they tend the sick and dying. Go with the long-distance lorry driver, the air pilot – all those on the night shift. Help us not to try to manage our lives without consulting you, Lord. Grant us your peace.

**April 29th**

> Wisdom is ofttimes nearer when we stoop
> Than when we soar.                    *Wordsworth*

**April 30th**

Since we have been thinking of work, it is perhaps appropriate to spend the last days of the month thinking of those whose labour has been remembered over the centuries. Today is the Feast Day of St Catherine of Siena, patron saint of Italy and Italian nurses. She nursed lepers, the terminally ill and those suffering from the plague, even digging the graves herself for the dying. She died at the same age as her Lord, just thirty-three. One time, during severe trial she asked, 'O my Saviour and Lord, why did you leave me when I was so sorely tried?' His reply was, 'My child, I have been with you all along. I was in your heart throughout.'

# MAY

*April is a promise that May is bound to keep.*

*Hal Borland*

*All things seem possible in May.* *Edwin Way Teale*

**May 1st**

MAY EVERY DAY BEGIN WITH SPACE

If only I knew
How to slow down and stop,
To rest half-way up
And not at the top.

If only I knew
How to make worries cease,
Knew something of healing
And living in peace.

If I could just see
How simply absurd
Is my critical face
And my judgmental word.

If only I could
Live a life that is good
If only, if only,
If only I could!

So may every day
Begin with space
Enough to see
My Saviour's face.

May every hour
Possess within it
The space to live
A prayerful minute.

And may I find
From night's alarms
The space within
My Saviour's arms.

I wish that I could
For everyone's sake
Discover some way
To undo each mistake.

If only I could
When my mind sees red
Allow that I should
Be laughing instead.

If only I knew
When I should be meek
Or when to be bold
And stand up and speak.

If only I could
Say my prayers as I should.
If only, if only,
If only I could.

So may every day
Begin with space
Enough to see
My Saviour's face.

May every hour
Possess within it
The space to live
A prayerful minute.

And may I find
From night's alarms
The space within
My Saviour's arms.                    *Frank Topping*

## May 2nd

Matthew Arnold once wrote of 'this strange disease of modern
life with its sick hurry'. He is reputed to have died of a heart
attack, running for a train!

## May 3rd

Some of my grandchildren gave me a small present, and the writing on the cover was even better than the gift. 'A grandmother is a dispenser of treats, a supplier of cuddles, a teacher of patience, and an underminer of parental decisions.'

## May 4th

Dominic Behan, the writer, once said that he had an occasional breakdown, to save him from going round the bend. And another writer, whose name I have forgotten, said that dreaming permits each and every one of us to be quietly and safely insane every night of our lives.

## May 5th

Once I asked my young class to use some words they had just learnt to spell. When it came to the word 'oracle', one lad wrote, 'I don't know why it is that every time I ask my Dad about something, he says, "We'll have to consult the oracle." And then he goes and asks my Mum!'

## May 6th

The heavens tell out the glory of God,
the vault of the earth reveals his handiwork. . . .
The law of the LORD is perfect and revives the soul.
    The LORD's instruction never fails. It makes the simple
      wise.
The precepts of the LORD are right and rejoice the heart.
    The commandment of the LORD shines clear
      and gives light to the eyes.
    The fear of the LORD is pure and abides for ever.
The LORD's decrees are true and righteous every one.

*Psalm 19:1, 7–9 (NEB)*

## May 7th

AN OLD CELTIC BLESSING

This day is Your love-gift to me.
This dawn I take it from Your hand.
Make me busy in Your service
    throughout its hours,
Yet not so busy that I cannot sing a happy song.

And may the South wind blow its tenderness through my heart
   so that I bear myself gently towards all.
And may the sunshine of it pass into my thoughts,
   so that each shall be a picture of Your thought
     Noble and bright.

## May 8th

I have a very vivid memory from my childhood which continually surfaces, dredged up like the fragments of a dream. There is a large, comfortable, warm and reassuring presence seated in the corner of a living room, surrounded by her numerous children and even more numerous grandchildren, of whom I was one. She was very different from the modern, trendy, active grandmothers, for in my memory she seems permanently immobile, but not silent. I don't remember much of what she said, but I can remember often playing on the floor at her feet with the latest jigsaw or toy, as she sang quietly one of the old gospel hymns. She was undisturbed by our play, but periodically, without being told, we would lapse into near silence, with only the softest of whispers, for my grandmother had lifted the skirt of her voluminous apron, and had placed it over her head. Here was someone at prayer. Not a gospel hymn any more, but one of her beloved psalms. Rich with that memory I have always since associated prayer with the psalms.

## May 9th

If you have any difficulty concentrating during prayer time, I give you a little plan I worked out years back, when I thought of my grandmother singing her psalms softly in her private sanctuary behind the folds of her apron draped over her head. I used the word PSALM as a crutch. P for Praise: S for Surrender: A for Asking: L for Listening and M for meditation. Much later I was fascinated to learn that the psalmist who wrote Psalms 111 and 112 used a mnemonic as well. Each of those psalms consists of 22 phrases beginning with successive letters of the Hebrew alphabet.

## May 10th

     Dear Lord, please grant the thing I ask
     If you'd be glad about it,
     But if you think it's not for me
     Then help me do without it.

This is really just a popped up version of an old prayer of Julian of Norwich, whose early fifteenth-century writings have become so popular. Her version was:

Lord, you know what I want, if it be your will that I can have it. If it is not your will, good Lord, do not be displeased, for I want nothing that you do not want.

## May 11th

On the day that our firstborn declared that he would not repeat a prayer after Mummy or Daddy but would say one 'his very own self', there was at first a tense silence. Then he enquired, 'How are you getting along today, dear God?' Since then he has composed many prayers, some of which I will leave with you later in this book. Another of our children, after asking God to bless numerous relatives and friends, always finished with, 'And even bless your own self, dear God.'

## May 12th

How often in spontaneous prayer in public have you heard someone try to get across something to the listeners, whilst he pretends to talk to God. I suppose that was why Jesus was so hard on the Pharisee who thanked God he was not like the poor sinner. We all do it at times, and I was greatly amused one day, just after I had arrived to see my small grandchildren, when one of them asked to be allowed to say Grace. She thanked God for everything on the table – the ham, the cheese, the butter, the milk, the salads. And then she said, 'And I even thank you for the Scottish honey Granny has just brought, though you know I don't like it.' As good a way as any, she thought, to pre-empt the admonition, 'Come now, and eat this up. It's very good for you.'

## May 13th

O God, thou art my God; early will I seek thee: my soul thirsteth for thee, my flesh longeth for thee in a dry and thirsty land, where no water is; to see thy power and thy glory, so as I have seen thee in the sanctuary. Because thy lovingkindness is better than life, my lips shall praise thee. Thus will I bless thee while I live; I will lift up my hands in thy name. My soul shall be satisfied as with marrow and fatness; and my mouth shall praise thee with joyful lips: when I remember thee upon my bed, and meditate on thee in the night watches. Because thou hast been my help, therefore in the shadow of thy wing will I rejoice. My soul followeth hard after thee: thy right hand upholdeth me.                    *Psalm 63:1–8 (AV)*

## May 14th

A PRAYER FOR THE NIGHT

May our sleeping
be a prayer of trust, O God.

May our sins be all forgiven;
And may we, too, freely forgive
and bless all who have hurt us.
But help us! We cannot alone!

May your angels guard the helpless and innocent.
May darkness bring healing to broken souls.
May the dying depart in peace.

May our sleeping
be a prayer of trust, O Lord.                    *Michael Urch*

## May 15th

During the worst period of 'the troubles' in Northern Ireland, a young nun called Catherine was killed by an IRA bomb. One of her colleagues was interviewed about her. She described her happy spirit and jollity, and she told how Catherine had placed in her room a little plaque with a prayer which she prayed at the beginning of each day. It went something like this: 'Lord, don't let anything happen to me today, which you and I together can't lick.' Sometimes we wait for a crisis to happen before we appeal to God – as it has been said, there are not many atheists on board when a ship is going down. But Catherine took hold of God in anticipation of crises. The innermost value of prayer is the search of the soul for God, and the wonder is that he enters, by a private door, the soul of each individual who seeks him.

## May 16th

The Irish writer Brendan Behan's last words were to the nun who was attending him. 'May God bless you, sister. And may all your sons become bishops!'

## May 17th

Marshall Hall was a famous turn-of-the-century barrister, noted for his oratory, clarity and insight. When he was terminally ill, he said, 'About the afterlife, my knowledge is nil. My belief strong. My hope infinite.'

## May 18th

> The tongues of dying men
> Enforce attention, like deep harmony.
> Where words are scarce, they are seldom spent in vain
> For they breathe truth that breathe their words in pain.
>
> *Shakespeare:* Richard II

## May 19th

Blaise Pascal lived in the seventeenth century, and he invented a calculating machine, a syringe and a hydraulic press. He once apologised about writing a long letter, saying he simply did not have the time to make it shorter. Those of us who indulge our love of writing can understand the paradox in those words.

'Brevity is the soul of wit.'                    *Shakespeare:* Hamlet.

## May 20th

Let not your heart be troubled: ye believe in God, believe also in me. In my Father's house are many mansions: if it were not so, I would have told you. I go to prepare a place for you. And if I go and prepare a place for you, I will come again, and receive you unto myself; that where I am, there ye may be also. And whither I go ye know, and the way ye know. Thomas saith unto him, Lord, we know not whither thou goest; and how can we know the way? Jesus saith unto him, I am the way, the truth, and the life: no man cometh unto the Father, but by me.

*John 14:1–6 (AV)*

**May 21st**

For everything there is a season;
our joys soar and fall,
our sorrows deepen and soften,
for every death a birth,
for every waking a falling asleep.
Our lives are fragile and beautiful,
our pilgrimage wonderful and frail.
Yet your lovingkindness is constant, O Lord,
your lovingkindness lasts for ever.

So we pray:
God of our beginning,
guide our way.
God of our being,
breathe within us.
God of our trusting,
save us faltering.
God of our hoping,
lead us from despair.
God of our longing,
let our hearts not grow cold.
God of our past,
let us never forget you.
God of our present,
be steadfastly with us.
God of our future,
welcome us home.
God of our living,
let us live in your presence.
God of our dying,
guard us in your peace.
God of our eternity,
bless us always.

*Michael Urch (based on Ecclesiastes 3:1–15)*

**May 22nd**

From time to time when I want to avail myself of some home-spun wisdom I go back to the Anna books by Fynn – the story of an extraordinary friendship with an extraordinary child. Anna was quite uninhibited when she spoke of her relationship with Mister God. And she also fostered relationships with people we might well shun. One of these was Millie who lived around Anna's area and was commonly called the Venus de Mile End. Anna said that she wished very much that Millie would know real, proper, sweet love. And when she wanted to visit people like Millie, Fynn's mother would say, 'If they are blind, give them your hand. If they are only in the dark, give them a candle.' And Fynn's mother also said that that candle could be called Anna.

The truth that God cares for each one of us is beautiful to contemplate, but sometimes difficult to believe. Sometimes we have to look at the faith of a child to understand how truly God cares.

**May 23rd**

In men whom men condemn as ill
I find so much of goodness still.
In men whom men pronounce divine
I find so much of sin and blot.
I do not care to draw a line
Between the two where God has not.

*Joaquin Miller*

**May 24th**

The heart that forgives an injury is like the perforated shell of an oyster which closes its wound with a pearl.

**May 25th**

If all the good people were clever
And all clever people were good
The world would be nicer than ever
We thought that it possibly could.
But alas it is seldom or never
The two hit it off as they should:
The good are so harsh on the clever
And the clever so rude to the good.

*Elizabeth Wordsworth*

**May 26th**

> If every man would mend a man
> Then all mankind were mended.

**May 27th**

Ye are the light of the world. A city that is set on an hill cannot be hid. Neither do men light a candle, and put it under a bushel, but on a candlestick; and it giveth light unto all that are in the house. Let your light so shine before men, that they may see your good works, and glorify your Father which is in heaven.                                     *Matthew 5:14–16 (AV)*

I am the light of the world: he that followeth me shall not walk in darkness, but shall have the light of life.          *John 8:12 (AV)*

**May 28th**

Lord God, we cannot hide from you the things that we try to hide from ourselves and others. Some of us are made blind and isolated by our failings. We desperately need someone to take hold of us and lead us. Some of us are fumbling about in the dark and desperately need someone to provide us with light. When we seek the darkness rather than the light, in our perverse and foolish ways, Lord, challenge us by your presence. Illumine our lives and then give us grace not to keep that light to ourselves, but to take it wherever our daily duties take us, so that others will be enlightened as well.

**May 29th**

When I was a child, it was expected of us that we would learn by heart the ten commandments. Nowadays we wryly say that the only commandment you need to remember is 'Thou shalt not be found out'. John Bunyan, all those years ago, made a rhyme to enable people to remember the commandments, and in the last century a version of it was commonly taught to children:

Have no other gods but me
And to no image bow the knee.
Take not the name of God in vain.
Do not the Sabbath day profane.
Honour thy father and mother too
And see that thou no murder do.
Abstain from thoughts and deeds unclean
And steal not, though thy state be mean.
Of false report bear not the blot.
What is thy neighbour's, covet not.

**May 30th**
A couple of choir boys were in trouble with the vicar. One was
punching the other during the sermon, because of a minor dis-
pute over a piece of chewing gum. The vicar chastised them
later, and in the way of a good pastor suggested this was no way
to behave in the House of God. He said they should make their
peace with each other by apologising. The one who had done
the thumping said, 'Well, I'm really sorry I hit you inside the
church. I should have waited till I got you outside.'

**May 31st**
At the end of the month, it might be salutary to think of the
epitaph on this date in 1771, for someone called Arabella
Young:

> Beneath this stone
> A lump of clay
> Lies Arabella Young
> Who on the 31st of May,
> 1771
> Began to hold her tongue.

As the saying goes, 'They don't write them like that any more.'

# JUNE

*No price is set on the lavish summer.*
*June may be had by the poorest comer.*

*J. R. Lowell*

## June 1st

### A NAVAHO BLESSING

Creator God,
 With your feet I walk
  I walk with your limbs
   I carry forth your body,
For me your mind thinks,
 Your voice speaks for me.
Beauty is before me,
 And beauty is behind me,
  Above and below me hovers the beautiful,
  I am surrounded by it
   I am immersed in it.

In my youth I am aware of it
 And in my old age I will walk quietly
  the beautiful trail.

## June 2nd

It has been said that the first ecologists were the American Indians. Certainly they have displayed a kinship with nature, and a reverence for God's creation, from which we can learn. According to one Hopi Indian belief, there is but one race, the human race, which has been divided into two groups – one light-skinned, and one dark-skinned. The belief is that God gave the gift of perception, the gift of knowing to the dark-skinned. And to the light, he gave the gift of recording and the gift of doing. The Hopi Indian belief is that only when the two peoples can unite at a centre and share their gifts, will each receive a greater gift than either alone can give.

## June 3rd

Here is a Poor Man's Grace to remember next time we hesitate about giving, when asked to help feed the starving of our world:

> Heavenly Father, bless us
> And keep us all alive.
> There's ten of us to dinner
> And not enough for five. *Unattributed*

## June 4th

The Poor Clares were founded by Clare Offreducio, who became known as St Clare of Assisi. She gave up a wealthy family to found a community which embraced the strictest poverty. But she maintained her initial love for music and all of the splendour of nature. When people tried to get her to relax the very strict rules of absolute poverty she replied, 'Can a heart which possesses God really be called poor?'

## June 5th

Contemplating beauty can be a worshipful experience. But we often must leave it behind to face the starker realities of life. C. S. Lewis once described sunlight glinting through the leaves of trees in a silver birch wood as 'patches of God-light in the wood of our experience'. We feel the freshness of the morning, but that does not make us fresh and pure. It can only create within us a desire to reach out for God. Our individual woods and the paths through them are as different as we are in personality and circumstance, but patches of God-light we shall surely find.

## June 6th

Thus speaks the LORD who is God,
  he who created the skies and stretched them out,
  who fashioned the earth and all that grows in it,
who gave breath to its people,
  the breath of life to all who walk upon it:
I, the LORD, have called you with righteous purpose
    and taken you by the hand;
  I have formed you, and appointed you
    to be a light to all peoples,

a beacon for the nations,
to open eyes that are blind,
to bring captives out of prison,
out of the dungeons where they lie in darkness.
I am the LORD; the LORD is my name.     *Isaiah 42:5–8 (NEB)*

## June 7th

Here is an old Celtic benediction, bringing peace or wholeness
– which is I think the true meaning of 'benediction':

> Deep peace of the running wave to you
> Deep peace of the flowing air to you
> Deep peace of the quiet earth to you
> Deep peace of the shining stars to you
> Deep peace of the Son of peace to you.

## June 8th

I know I am very fortunate to live in an area where it is rela-
tively easy to escape the throng and to climb a hill or a mountain and in doing so to get thoughts unravelled. I'm not much
good now at high mountains, but I do know what is meant by
'mountain exhilaration'. So did George Adam Smith, who was a
well-known theologian. Once he had waited several days to
climb a difficult peak in Switzerland. Blizzards, gales and mists
delayed the expedition. Later, as they achieved the summit, the
guide who had steered Smith to his goal stood back to allow
Smith to be the first to savour the wonderful view awaiting
them. Smith, unaware that a fierce gale was blowing up the
other side of the mountain, rushed up the last few paces, until
the guide, with his wealth of experience, called out, 'On your
knees, Sir! On your knees! You are not safe there unless you
are on your knees!' Standing on any pinnacle in life can most
certainly give us a sense of elation, but the true perspective will
only come when we are safely and in all humility on our knees.

**June 9th**

> I see His blood upon the rose
> And in the stars the glory of His eyes,
> His body gleams amid eternal snows,
> His tears fall from the skies.
>
> I see His face in every flower;
> The thunder and the singing of the birds
> Are but His voice – and carven by His power
> Rocks are His written words.
>
> All pathways by His feet are worn,
> His strong heart stirs the ever-beating sea,
> His crown of thorns is twined with every thorn,
> His cross is every tree.                    *Joseph Plunkett*

**June 10th**

My friend, Archy the cockroach, whom I know through the writings of Don Marquis, said that moths were a bit like human beings used to be, before they became too civilised. They would rather be part of beauty for one instant and then cease to exist, than to exist for ever and never be a part of beauty. Fortunately we can learn how to be both, and whoever has helped us to that understanding deserves our lasting gratitude.

**June 11th**

There's a little African story about a conversation between the millipede and the spider:

Millipede: My dear, did you know that human beings must be deaf? When I stamp my thousand feet, they cannot even hear one of them.
Spider: Really! And did I never tell you that they are blind as well? When I've finished spinning my new house, they will walk right through it.

**June 12th**

Child to Mother: My shoes are hurting me.
Mother: No wonder! You've got them on the wrong feet.
Outraged child: But these are the only feet I've got!

## June 13th

Look at the birds of the air; they do not sow and reap and store in barns, yet your heavenly Father feeds them. You are worth more than all the birds! Is there a man among you who by anxious thought can add a foot to his height? And why be anxious about clothes? Consider how the lilies grow in the fields; they do not work, they do not spin; and yet, I tell you, even Solomon in all his splendour was not attired like one of these.

*Matthew 6:26–29 (NEB)*

## June 14th

O Lord God, keep us wholly sensitive to the wonder and beauty and glory that surround us. Give us a sense of reverence for all your creation. In viewing that part of it which has become familiar to our eyes and ears, may we ever guard against the familiar becoming the neglected. We especially ask you to help us daily to appreciate those we say we love, but whom so often we take for granted. Empower us to use the earthly span you have given us for your glory and your eternal purpose.

## June 15th

A few years back, just about this time of year, I was on Simskäla, a lovely little island in the archipelago of Åland, lying in the Baltic Sea halfway between Stockholm and Helsinki. Later, that beautiful but cruel sea became the grave of the ship *Estonia* and many of its passengers in the autumn of 1994. It also had snatched in earlier years and on three different occasions the husband and the two sons of Anni Blomqvist, whose home was on Simskäla. She was a well-known local writer who had depicted movingly the hardships of life in those Finnish islands. I had just been visiting her recent grave on a neighbouring island and wanted to see where her books had been written. The view from her study window that summer's day was exquisite as I looked across a very deep blue and calm sea dotted about with its skerries.

Anni's home was modest and even spartan, but it was easy to see that she had been a woman who had communed with God. Here was her Bible, and there on the walls were the biblical texts which had sustained her through her many sorrows. As I stood at her desk where she had placed the photo of the son who had recently drowned, I could not help but feel the agony of her grief, for she had placed beside the photo her son's watch. Despite the lapse of time between his drowning and the finding of his body, the watch when found was still ticking accurately away. I was moved by the irony of it. The relentless sea had given back to her this disposable, material object, having taken from her all else that she treasured.

I have never been able to read a word that Anni Blomqvist has written, for though translated into other languages, her books are not yet in English. But her life has touched mine, as have her sorrows. As Charles Reade said in his opening words of *The Cloister and the Hearth*, 'Not a day passes over the earth but men and women of no great note do great deeds, speak great words and suffer noble sorrows.'

## June 16th

### LAMENT FOR HATHIMODA, ABBESS OF GANDESHEIM

> Thou hast come safe to port
> I still at sea
> The light is on thy head
> Darkness in me
> Pluck thou in Heaven's fields
> Violet and rose
> While I strew flowers that will thy vigil keep
> Where thou dost sleep, love
> In thy last repose.
>
> *Ninth century; translated by Helen Waddell*

## June 17th

Certain things cannot be seen except with eyes that have wept.

*Veuillot*

Suffering is evil, but the alchemy of divine grace and human courage can turn it into gold.    *Carroll-Abbing*

## June 18th

Robert Louis Stevenson on his travels met an old woman who used to frighten the natives of Vailima because she had discovered the power of ventriloquism. When Stevenson was dying, he recalled her and said to a friend:

'All the old women in the world might talk with their mouths shut and not frighten you and me. But there are plenty of other things that frighten us badly. And if we only knew about them, we should find them no more worth to be feared than any old woman talking with her mouth shut. And the names of some of these things are Death and Pain and Sorrow.'

## June 19th

A lion chased me up a tree
And I greatly enjoyed the view from the top.

*Confucius*

## June 20th

I have chosen these short Bible readings because they were Anni Blomqvist's favourite verses:

The eternal God is thy refuge, and underneath are the ever-lasting arms. *Deuteronomy 33:27 (AV)*

Young men may grow weary and faint,
even in their prime, they may stumble and fall;
but those who look to the LORD will win new strength,
they will grow wings like eagles;
they will run and not be weary,
they will march on and never grow faint.

*Isaiah 40:30–31 (NEB)*

## June 21st

Lord God, we pray for those who go down to the sea in ships and whose business takes them into deep waters. Be their and our strong refuge. And for those who feel they are drowning in a sea of grief because of the loss of those they love, give again the assurance that 'life is eternal, and love is immortal, and death is only a horizon, and a horizon is nothing more than the limit of our sight'.

## June 22nd

Sir Basil Spence, who designed Coventry Cathedral, said the designing of it was like an act of worship. Under a local anaesthetic in his dentist's he passed out and had a wonderful dream of the completed cathedral, with even the organ playing beautiful music. He saw also the stained glass windows at the rear of the edifice, and from this dream he gained many ideas for his design. Later, leafing over his son's *Geographical Magazine*, he saw an enlarged colour photo of a fly's eye. He used that design for the ceiling.

## June 23rd

The patron saint of architects is St Thomas or, as he is more often called, Doubting Thomas. There are various legends about how he came to be their patron saint, but the one I like best is this.

Thomas was sent as a missionary to India, and there Gundaphorus, an Indian king, gave him money to build a palace. He refused to do this, giving the money instead to the many poor. When challenged about it, he said he had thus 'created a superb palace in heaven'. The patron saints each have a symbol, and that for Thomas is a builder's square.

## June 24th

We shall have to evolve
    problem solvers galore
Since each problem we solve
    creates ten problems more.

## June 25th

And I say, that life is indeed darkness,
    save when there is urge
And all urge is blind
    save when there is knowledge
And all knowledge is vain
    save when there is work
And all work is empty
    save when there is love
And when you work with love
    you bind yourself to yourself
And to one another
    and to God.

*Kahlil Gibran*

## June 26th

As I was about to write something for this day, I was talking to a passer-by about some deplorable weather we were having. I said we'd best just get on with it, since there's nothing we can do to alter it. 'A good job too,' he said. 'If the politicians got their hands on it, things would be even worse.' That brought to mind the following anonymous nineteenth-century rhyme:

### GASBAGS

I'm thankful that the sun and moon
Are both hung up so high
That no pretentious hand can stretch
And pull them from the sky.
If they were not, I have no doubt
That some reforming ass
Would recommend to take them down
And light the world by gas.

## June 27th

Whosoever heareth these sayings of mine, and doeth them, I will liken him unto a wise man, which built his house upon a rock: and the rain descended, and the floods came, and the winds blew, and beat upon that house; and it fell not for it was founded upon a rock. And every one that heareth these sayings of mine, and doeth them not, shall be likened unto a foolish man, which built his house upon the sand: and the rain descended, and the floods came, and the winds blew, and beat upon that house; and it fell: and great was the fall of it.

*Matthew 7:24–27 (AV)*

Except the LORD build the house, they labour in vain that build it.           *Psalm 127:1 (AV)*

## June 28th

One of the best-loved prayers in the world was written in the sixteenth century by St Ignatius Loyola. After an injury when he served in the Spanish army, fighting the French, he started reading about the life of Christ. He became so devoted and spiritual that the rest of his life was spent with the dedication we find in the following prayer:

Teach us, good Lord,
To serve you as you deserve,
To give and not to count the cost,
To fight and not to heed the wounds,
To toil and not to seek for rest,
To labour and not to ask for any reward
Save that of knowing that we do your will.

## June 29th

We are now at the middle of the year, having passed midsummer, when we expect to allow ourselves to go a little mad and to shed some of the worries and tedium of the early part of the year. So here's a little mirthful rhyme written over a century ago by J. B. Naylor:

### CONSCIENCE

King David and King Solomon led merry, merry lives
With many, many lady friends and many, many wives;
But when old age crept over them, with many, many qualms
King Solomon wrote Proverbs and King David wrote the
    Psalms.

## June 30th

### A SUNDIAL MOTTO

Time is
Too Slow for those who Wait
Too Swift for those who Fear
Too Long for those who Grieve
Too Short for those who Rejoice
  But for those who Love
    Time is not.

# JULY

*Oh, the summer night*
*Has a smile of light*
*As she sits on a sapphire throne.*     *B. W. Procter*

## July 1st

Someone has said that the Lord's Prayer is easy to commit to memory, but exceedingly difficult to learn by heart. Sometimes it is good to see it interpreted by someone of another culture so that we can meet again some of its challenge.

THE LORD'S PRAYER: AMERICAN-INDIAN VERSION

Great Spirit, whose tepee is the sky
  And whose hunting ground is the earth
    Mighty and fearful are you called.
Ruler over storms, over men and birds and beasts
    Have your way over all,
    Over earthways and over skyways.

Find us this day our meat and corn,
  That we may be strong and brave.
And put aside from us our wicked ways
As we put aside the bad works of those who do us wrong.

And let us not have such troubles
  As lead us into crooked roads,
  But keep us from all evil,
For yours is all that is –
  The earth and the sky,
  The streams and the hills,
    The valleys,
    The stars, the moon and the sun,
    And all that live and breathe.

Wonderful, Shining, Mighty Spirit.

## July 2nd

Certain thoughts are prayers. There are moments when, whatever the attitude of the body, the soul is on its knees.

*Victor Hugo:* Les Misérables

75

## July 3rd

I suppose the hardest part of the Lord's Prayer is the acceptance of, in the words of the American-Indian version, the need to put away the bad works of those who have done us wrong. We like to get our own back in some way or other. There is the humorous story of the three magistrates in the South of England who were arrested at different times for speeding. They wangled it so that they would try each other's cases and each would plead for leniency. The first one fined the second one £50 and admonished him. The second one fined the third one the same amount and gave the same admonishment. But when the third came to try the first, the fine was £100 and a severe reprimand. The first one challenged him about his harsh dealings, and he replied, 'Well, by the time I tried your case I had begun to think that I'd have to show this fellow a lesson. After all, this kind of thing is happening too often these days. Yours was the third case which came up this morning!'

## July 4th

Don't walk in front of me: I may not follow.
Don't walk behind me: I may not lead.
Walk beside me, and be my friend.      *Albert Camus*

## July 5th

Fritz Schumacher was the author of *Small is Beautiful*. When someone referred to him as a crank, the memory of having to use a crank to get your car started was still green.

He said: 'Someone called me a crank. I don't mind at all. A crank is a low-cost, low-capital tool. It can be used on a moderately small scale. It is non-violent. But it makes revolutions.'

## July 6th

Be generous to one another, tender-hearted, forgiving one another as God in Christ forgave you.

In a word, as God's dear children, try to be like him, and live in love as Christ loved you, and gave himself up on your behalf as an offering and sacrifice whose fragrance is pleasing to God.
*Ephesians 4:32 and 5:1–2 (NEB)*

## July 7th

This prayer was written on a scrap of paper by a woman prisoner in Ravensbrück concentration camp:

O Lord, remember not only the men and women of goodwill, but also those of ill-will. But do not only remember the suffering they have inflicted on us. Remember the fruits we bought, thanks to this suffering. Our comradeship, our loyalty, our humility, our courage, our generosity, the greatness of heart which has grown out of all this. And when they come to judgment, let all the fruits that we have borne be their forgiveness.

## July 8th

When I was staying at a motel in the Grampian Mountains in Australia, right at the heart of koala country, we were wakened each night by fierce roaring and grunting and squealing. Before those evening disturbances I had always had the illusion that koalas were soft, cuddly, gentle creatures. But I looked out each night to see the fierce males fighting over a female. When I saw them asleep high up in the trees during the day, again looking cuddly and innocent, I thought of Konrad Lorenz, who had discovered quite a few fallacies in our popular beliefs about animals. A dove, generally regarded as most docile, can be murderous at times, whereas a wolf, generally regarded as the fiercest of animals, can be the most merciful. Lorenz has said that if one wolf attacks another and the attacked one places himself alongside his opponent, and offers the most vulnerable part of his body – the back of his neck – the attacking wolf finds it impossible to strike and a truce is declared. Lorenz reminds us, in telling this in *King Solomon's Ring*, that the Homeric warrior, when he wanted to yield, discarded his helmet and shield, and fell on his knees, inclining his head, so that he was seemingly making it more easy for the enemy to kill him. In reality he was preventing him from doing so. Lorenz said that this should give us a new insight into the difficult words in Luke 6:29, 'And unto him that smiteth thee on the one cheek offer also the other.'

## July 9th

I have been told that in the old Jewish tradition if one had to go to the aid of an enemy and a friend at the same time, one was obliged to help the enemy first. That way, I guess, you would end up having two friends instead of one. I have not seen or heard of any evidence of that tradition still being carried on, though Proverbs 25 had something to say about heaping coals of fire on an enemy's head by feeding him when hungry, and giving him water to drink when thirsty.

## July 10th

There's the classic story of the man who complained that his wife was always reminding him of his past mistakes.

'I thought you told me that you'd forgive and forget,' he said.

'Well, so I have,' she answered. 'It's just that I don't want you to forget that I've forgiven and forgotten.'

Forgiveness is not, and should never be regarded as, easy. Forgetting may be well-nigh impossible. Indeed sometimes it may be essential to remember, rather than forget, the very deeds that need forgiveness. We as human beings should never forget or gloss over the depravity which man is capable of. Calvary, the Holocaust, Enniskillen, Dunblane, Tasmania. Forgiveness is not just shutting out the past and forgetting. It is an empowered form of giving. It is a taking stock of all the wounds that have been inflicted and setting about the healing process which will acknowledge the scars, but will also desire to aim at wholeness again, rather than a reopening of hurts.

## July 11th

Mark Twain said it wasn't the Scriptures that he failed to understand which worried him. He was more exercised about the ones he did understand.

## July 12th

When I was living in Northern Ireland in the sixties it was reported that a minister of one of the larger churches in the Province was addressing a full congregation of Orangemen meeting for their annual service. He hadn't seen such a crowd for ages. His eyes moved round the circle of the gallery, and from corner to corner of the ground floor. The silence was deafening as they waited for his first words. Then they came.

'Well, brethren, now that I've got you all here, I might as well wish you a merry Christmas, for there are some of you I do not expect to find within these walls again before then.'

Sometimes we make an agony out of our religion, when a touch of merriment can bring a stab of truth and a hint of glory into our midst.

## July 13th

Ye have heard that it hath been said, Thou shalt love thy neighbour, and hate thine enemy. But I say unto you, Love your enemies, bless them that curse you, do good to them that hate you, and pray for them which despitefully use you, and persecute you; that ye may be the children of your Father which is in heaven: for he maketh his sun to rise on the evil and on the good, and sendeth rain on the just and on the unjust. For if ye love them which love you, what reward have ye? do not even the publicans the same? And if ye salute your brethren only, what do ye more than others? do not even the publicans so? Be ye therefore perfect, even as your Father which is in heaven is perfect.                    *Matthew 5:43–48 (AV)*

## July 14th

A PRAYER FOR INTEGRITY

Lord, we cannot hide from you
what we hide even from ourselves;
though how we try!
Help us then to dare to pray,
to risk the pain,
to find ourselves
as found by you, in Christ.          *Michael Urch*

## July 15th

A few years ago I was in conversation with a young Swede who had blown off his hand in a laboratory prank when he was about seventeen. He worked in a car factory in Gothenburg, and I suspect he hated it, for he travelled far each evening after work to what we in Scotland would call his croft. There he would indulge his passion for gardening, classical music and philosophising. Out of the blue one evening he said something which I still wrestle with.

'I am convinced,' he said, 'that everything we do in life, we do for ourselves.'

I mentioned Mother Theresa and some other saintly folk who had given up all that we know of life's luxuries.

'But,' he said, 'they were obeying an inner compulsion. They were fulfilling their own need, for they could not have lived with themselves had they done other.'

I was reminded then of a woman who had given money to a homeless teenager, and he rejected it. She said honestly, 'I guess he didn't need my charity as much as I needed to shower it on him.'

Many times we realise that we have mixed motives for doing good. It's pretty easy to detect when it's merely a sense of duty, and we can all feel threatened by that kind of goodness. But when you meet the real kind of saint – well, they're irresistible!

## July 16th
I think I would have enjoyed very much being in the company of the sixteenth-century saint called Teresa of Avila. Though she founded the Barefooted Carmelites, which was a pretty austere order, she revealed a keen sense of humour when she said that she hoped the Lord would deliver her from 'sullen saints and silly devotions'.

## July 17th
Things weren't a lot different in some respects in the sixteenth century from how they are today. One thing that Teresa of Avila thought was expedient was to limit her convents to twenty women, for she said that she had learnt from experience what a house full of women could be like. The main difference today is that a statement like that might not be quite politically correct!

## July 18th
Christ has no body here on earth but yours. He has only your hands to do his work, and to bless others. He has only your feet to go about his world, doing good. It is through your eyes that his love can look out to the troubled world. Christ has no body now on earth but yours.                     *Teresa of Avila (adapted)*

Michel Quoist puts the same idea in a more modern context when, in one of his prayers, he offers himself to God as a sub-contractor.

## July 19th

I believe that in Britain, the Archbishops and the Bishop of Durham hold their office by 'Divine Providence'. All others hold theirs by 'Divine Permission'. Bishop Hensley Henson said once that at times he almost came to believe that some bishops held their office by 'Divine Inadvertence'.

## July 20th

Comfort each other and strengthen each other, just as you are already doing. Acknowledge those who are working hard for you for Christ's sake and hold highly in esteem those who are your leaders in the Lord's work. Try as far as possible to live peaceably with each other. Admonishment is sometimes needed for the careless, but support those who may be weak and be very patient with all.

*1 Thessalonians 5:11–14 (NEB, adapted)*

## July 21st

This prayer is supposed to have been written in the seventeenth century. I like to think it is actually late sixteenth century when it might well have been written by Teresa of Avila when she was advancing in years.

ON AGEING: A NUN'S PRAYER

Lord, thou knowest better than I do that I am growing old and will one day be old. Keep me from getting talkative and particularly from the fatal habit of thinking that I must say something on every subject and every occasion.

Release me from trying to straighten out everyone's affairs. Make me thoughtful, but not moody: helpful but not curious. With my vast store of wisdom, it seems a pity not to use it all, but thou knowest, Lord, that I want a few friends at the end.

Keep my mind free from the recital of endless details. Give me wings to get to the point. Seal my lips from my many aches and pains. They are increasing and my love of rehearsing them is becoming sweeter as the years go by. I ask for grace enough to listen to the tales of others' pains. Help me to endure them with patience.

Teach me the glorious lesson that occasionally it is possible I am mistaken. Keep me reasonably sweet. I do not want to be a saint. Some of them are very hard to live with. But a sour old woman is one of the crowning works of the devil. Help me to extract all possible fun out of life. There are so many funny things around, and I do not want to miss any.

## July 22nd
One little fellow I know had a great struggle getting his sums right. No matter how hard he tried, he just couldn't manage numbers. Then one day he told me with a radiant smile that he had got everything right that day. I congratulated him, and said, 'Now, how did you manage that?'

'Well,' he said, 'today I marked them all myself!'

We know that urge, don't we? We want to feel good about ourselves, and we want others to feel good about us too. So we're not above cheating a little bit here and there. Now there's a dilemma here, and a tension, for nobody should demolish in either themselves or others the sense of worth. Yet we need to face up to our individual frailties and limitations. That little lad had other talents, especially in personality. And since we're on the matter of arithmetic, and multiplying of talents and so on, we might as well remember that no matter how often you try to multiply nothing, you'll still end up with nothing. That young man would be helped out by his calculator in days to come, so he needn't have worried too much.

We are all an extraordinary work of nature, and who can tell what we may have the power to become when we liberate ourselves of false expectations of ourselves and others.

## July 23rd
Lewis Carroll has his Mock Turtle telling of his study of the various branches of Arithmetic. He said he had studied Ambition, Distraction, Uglification and Derision.

Wouldn't it be best if we could all claim to be innumerate in three at least of these branches?

**July 24th**
Teacher to pupil: Where's the dot over the 'i' in that word?
Pupil: It's still inside my pencil!

**July 25th**
Dietrich Bonhoeffer was a German Lutheran pastor who was
an opponent of Nazism and was deeply involved in the German
Resistance movement. He was arrested and imprisoned in 1943
and hanged in 1945 at Flossenburg. In his *Letters and Papers
from Prison* which were published in 1953 he wrote:

Who am I? This or the other?
Am I one person and tomorrow another?
Am I both at once? A hypocrite before others,
And before myself a contemptible woebegone weakling?
Or is something within me like a beaten army
Fleeing in disorder from victory already achieved?

Who am I?
They mock me, these lonely questions of mine.
Whoever I am, thou knowest, O God, I am thine.

**July 26th**

He who knows not
   and knows not that he knows not
      is a fool!
Shun him.

He who knows not
   and knows that he knows not
      is ignorant.
Teach him.

He who knows
   and knows not that he knows
      is asleep.
Wake him.

He who knows
   and knows that he knows
      is a wise man.
Follow him.                               *Author unknown*

## July 27th

For I know whom I have believed, and am persuaded that he is able to keep that which I have committed unto him against that day.                    *2 Timothy 1:12 (AV)*

Who shall separate us from the love of Christ? Shall tribulation, or distress, or persecution, or famine, or nakedness, or peril, or sword? . . . Nay, in all these things we are more than conquerors through him that loved us. For I am persuaded, that neither death, nor life, nor angels, nor principalities, nor powers, nor things present, nor things to come, nor height, nor depth, nor any other creature, shall be able to separate us from the love of God, which is in Christ Jesus our Lord.

*Romans 8:35, 37–39 (AV)*

## July 28th

A PRAYER FOR THE MORNING

In stillness, as the day begins,
we give you thanks, O God,
for our sleeping and our waking.
Grant that we live today in hope,
trusting you more than ourselves,
loving each other within your love.
Keep us mindful of those whom the night distressed,
and for whom daylight is cold comfort.
And upon us all
may the peace of Christ rest,
for in his name we ask it.                    *Michael Urch*

## July 29th

Youth is for freedom and reform,
Maturity is for judicious compromise,
Old age for stability and repose.                    *Churchill*

## July 30th

This is an early poem of Sydney Carter's. It seems just as relevant today when we have the same worries about nuclear disasters, pesticides, the morality of some modern medical developments and so on and so on.

You who are seventeen
blame me because
the world is in a mess.

When I was seventeen
we talked about
the Treaty of Versailles.

And so we pass the buck
right back to Adam:
So let me

Ask in the name of
my small son
aged three

About insecticide,
the colour bar,
the H bomb
and the pill.

You will be thirty-one
when he is seventeen.
What (if anything)

Will you have done
to dodge the accusation
of my son?

## July 31st

That which your father hath bequeathed you
Earn anew if you would possess it.          *Goethe*

# AUGUST

*The paired butterflies are already yellow with August*
*over the grass in the West garden.*
*They hurt me. I grow older.*                    *Ezra Pound*

## August 1st
### TWENTY-THIRD PSALM: AMERICAN-INDIAN VERSION

The Great Father above a Shepherd is, and with him I want not.

He throws me out a rope, and the name of the rope is Love, and he draws me to where the grass is green, and the water is not dangerous, and I eat and lie down satisfied.

Sometimes my heart is very weak and falls down, but he lifts me up again and draws me into the good road. His name is Wonderful.

Sometime, it may be soon, it may be longer, it may be a long, long time, he will draw me into a place between the mountains. It is dark there, but I'll not draw back. I'll be afraid not, for it is there between the mountains that the Shepherd Chief will meet me, and the hunger that I felt all through this life will be satisfied. Sometimes he makes the love rope into a whip, but afterwards he gives me a staff to lean upon.

He spreads the table before me with all kinds of food. He puts his hand upon my head and all the tired is gone. My cup he fills until it is running over.

What I tell you is true: I lie not. These roads that are away ahead will stay with me through life. And afterwards I will go to live in the 'Big Tepee', and sit down with the Shepherd Chief for ever.

## August 2nd

This inscription was found written on the walls of a cellar in Cologne in Germany, where the Jews had hidden from the Nazis:

> I believe in the sun, even when it is not shining.
> I believe in love, even when feeling it not.
> I believe in God, even when he is silent.

## August 3rd

> Let go.
> Let gratitude fill your heart.
> Let God guide.

## August 4th

Someone has said that preparing for church should feel as exciting as preparing for a date – only more so. Alas, sometimes it is a struggle to raise any excitement whatsoever. It is not all the fault of the minister, though he is often blamed, for we who proclaim our trust in God as found in Christ are the church too. Despite saying that, I find the following little verse worth repeating. It is called 'The Bishop's Last Orders'.

> Tell my priests when I am gone
> Over me to shed no tears,
> For I shall be no deader then
> Than they have been for years.     *Unattributed*

## August 5th

People who do not attend church, giving as the simple excuse that it is all really rather boring, say we should throw out a lot of the old, and bring in a lot of the popular culture of our age. Of course we need in the journey of life to get rid of our excess baggage, but that must be done judiciously and with the highest of motives. Change for change's sake alone can be disastrous. Dean Inge once said, 'A Church which marries the *spirit* of the age will be a widow in the next generation.' He was sometimes referred to as 'the Gloomy Dean'.

## August 6th

Whatsoever things are true, whatsoever things are honest, whatsoever things are just, whatsoever things are of good report; if there be any virtue, and if there be any praise, think on these things. ... I have learned in whatsoever state I am, therewith to be content. I know both how to be abased, and how to abound: every where and in all things I am instructed both to be full and to be hungry, both to abound and to suffer need. I can do all things through Christ which strengtheneth me. *Philippians 4:8, 11–13 (AV)*

## August 7th

Lord God,
You have put us in charge of your world.
Show us how to become good stewards.
Help us to take responsibility for waste, pollution, destruction, poverty, hunger and suffering.
Forgive us where we have misused what you have endowed us with.
Deepen our trust in you.
Lift our levels of perception
so that we can pray aright
for those who are serving Christ in places of conflict,
and in areas of plague and famine.
Give us grace to endure for the sake of all your needy people
and for love of Christ who bore all for us.

## August 8th

Sir Giles Gilbert Scott was the architect who won the competition for the design of the Liverpool Anglican Cathedral in 1903. It was the last such building in Gothic style. He also was the designer of the telephone kiosk and he was responsible for the rebuilding of the House of Commons after World War 2. Isn't it interesting that all these buildings had to take into account that they would be places where the human voice would be heard in one way or another? I find a little parable here.

There is the space where our voices are joined in worship and we expect to hear the voice of God.

There is the more private space where we are talking one to one, just as we need to do with our God.

What can I say about the House of Commons, where Parliament is summoned by the sovereign? It has at times its unedifying scenes and strange privileges, where you can actually get away with saying something which might be considered libellous outside its walls. The very freedom of our democracy allows us that. And the free will which God has given us means that we too are able in speech to be influential for good or ill.

**August 9th**
Lord Macaulay, eminent writer, who was a politician himself in the mid-nineteenth century, said, 'Many politicians of our time are in the habit of laying it down as a self-evident proposition, that no people ought to be free till they are fit to use their freedom. The maxim is worthy of the fool in the old story, who resolved not to go into the water till he had learnt to swim. If men are to wait for liberty till they become wise and good in slavery, they may indeed wait for ever.'

There is a part in *Chariots of Fire* (the film of Eric Liddell's story) where Harold Abrahams declares that if he cannot win in a race, he won't run. His coach replies, 'Unless you run, you can't win.'

**August 10th**
Lord Melbourne, the nineteenth-century Prime Minister, once said of Lord Macaulay, who served in his Cabinet, 'I wish I could be as sure about any one thing as Macaulay is about everything.'

> Those who always know what's best
> Are a universal pest.

**August 11th**
Mandela in his *Long Walk to Freedom* has many searching and sometimes humorous things to say. He tells of a minister in Cape Town, who thanked the Lord for his bounty and goodness, his mercy and concern. But he felt he had to take the liberty of reminding the Lord that some of his subjects were more down-trodden than others, and it sometimes seemed as if he weren't paying attention. He told the Lord that if he did not take the initiative in leading the black man to salvation, the black man must take the matter into his own hands.

**August 12th**

> I am not born for one corner.
> The whole world is my native land.
>
> *Seneca the Younger (6 BC–AD 65)*

**August 13th**

What things were gain to me, those I counted loss for Christ. Doubtless I count all things but loss for the excellency of the knowledge of Christ Jesus my Lord; for whom I have suffered the loss of all things . . . that I might win Christ, and be found in him, not having mine own righteousness, which is of the law, but that which is through the faith of Christ, the righteousness which is of God by faith; that I might know him, and the power of his resurrection, and the fellowship of his sufferings, being made conformable unto his death.  *Philippians 3:7–10 (AV)*

**August 14th**

TENTH-CENTURY IRISH PRAYER

> Christ the chaste, the cherished
> Searcher of the soul,
> Grant thy Holy Spirit
> To keep me in control.
> Rule my thoughts and feelings,
> You who brook no ill.
> Make me yours for ever.
> Bend me to your will.
> Grant me, Christ, to reach you;
> With you I long to be,
> For you're neither frail nor fickle
> Nor feeble-willed like me.

**August 15th**

Lord Bethell has told that his grandfather (in the days of stately homes) always hired his domestic staff according to 'the principle of eponymity' – their names had to fit. So it was that the chauffeur was a Mr Sparks; the gardener a Mr Trundle; the parlourmaid a Miss Kettle; the butler a Mr Crease – and the pantry boy, who was six feet tall, was called Longfellow. I wonder if the two parishes in a town not many miles from where I live also used 'the principle of eponymity' for until recently their ministers were Mr Heavenor and Mr Hellier.

And what do you make of this? Hosea was the son of Beeri and Ezekiel was the son of Buzi.

## August 16th
A smile is the shortest distance between two people.

## August 17th
Duke Ellington, the famous American jazz composer, was once turned down for the Pulitzer Prize. Someone asked him if he knew why, and he said that he guessed they didn't want him to become too famous when he was too young. He was by then in his sixties!

## August 18th
In times of impatience, I like to use the prayer of Bishop Frere, written for the Community of the Resurrection at Mirfield:

> My God, I can wait       if Thou uphold me
> I can endure             if Thou sustain me
> I can give up            if Thou reward me
> I gladly will do all     if Thou command me.
> O righteous Judge, Thou art both strong and patient
> I will be patient if Thou make me strong.

## August 19th
The Dean of Wells has a lovely story of one confirmation service he held. The new communicants were all allocated seats marked Reserved. They also had a name card to raise at the appropriate time, so that the Dean would call each correctly by name. One young lad held up the wrong card, the one marked *Reserved*. And so he was, remarked the Dean – being reserved for Christ!

## August 20th
Then Peter, filled with the Holy Ghost, said unto them, Ye rulers of the people, and elders of Israel, if we this day be examined of the good deed done to the impotent man, by what means he is made whole; be it known unto you all, and to all the people of Israel, that by the name of Jesus Christ of Nazareth, whom ye crucified, whom God raised from the dead, even by him doth this man stand here before you whole. This is the

stone which was set at nought of you builders, which is become the head of the corner. Neither is there salvation in any other: for there is none other name under heaven given among men, whereby we must be saved. *Acts 4:8–12 (AV)*

## August 21st

In the past sometimes a special kind of prayer, which I now sometimes call 'my fortress prayer', would be called a *lorica*. This was the Roman word for a certain piece of armour, and the special prayer was supposed to protect like armour, and save from evil. Here is an old lorica written by St Columba:

> Alone with none but thee, my God,
> I journey on my way.
> What need I fear
> When thou art near,
> O King of night and day?
> More safe am I within thy hand
> Than if a host around me stand.

## August 22nd

The Jewish people have a story about a rabbi who wished to see what heaven and hell really meant. He dreamt that he was taken to a room full of people wailing. They were sitting around a pot of soup, but were all starving as their spoons were so long that they could not eat with them. Then he was shown to another place which looked exactly the same except that everyone was well-fed and happy. They had discovered how to use the spoons to feed each other.

## August 23rd

> What is a Communist? One who has yearnings
> To share equal profits from unequal earnings.
> Be he idler or bungler, or both, he is willing
> To fork out his sixpence and pocket your shilling.
> *Ebenezer Elliot (1781–1849)*

**August 24th**

One of my friends took a photograph of a sign outside an Amish Settlement in the USA:

> In God we trust –
> Everyone else must pay cash!

**August 25th**

Mick in Ireland strutted around his village, boasting that he didn't believe all this stuff about heaven and hell. When he died, they dressed him up for the Irish wake, and as in olden times the villagers came to pay their respects. The parish priest, who had often been the butt of Mick's jokes, arrived, took a look and then said, 'Ach, sure Mick, there ye are now! All dressed up – and nowhere to go!'

**August 26th**

Man derides what he does not understand. *Goethe*

**August 27th**

Peace I leave with you, my peace I give unto you: not as the world giveth, give I unto you. Let not your heart be troubled, neither let it be afraid. Ye have heard how I said unto you, I go away, and come again unto you. If ye loved me, ye would rejoice, because I said, I go unto the Father: for my Father is greater than I. And now I have told you before it come to pass, that, when it is come to pass, ye might believe.

*John 14:27–29 (AV)*

**August 28th**

IN ANXIETY

Lord, we are so full of troubles,
real and imagined,
so easily given to pitying ourselves!
  We seldom realise
that perhaps you forgive us
more readily than we forgive ourselves.
In forgiveness, let us trust you.
And in trust, let us see
  which anxieties are real.
In your presence, let us face them,
  and take a step in courage.

*Michael Urch*


**August 29th**

Fred Hoyle, the famous astrophysicist, said that a world existing by accident is as likely as a whirlwind passing through a scrapyard and assembling a jumbo jet.


**August 30th**

My popular young school chaplain was intent on getting some of my youngsters to learn a lost art – the skill of finding their way through the library of books making up the Bible. He set them a puzzle one day. On one side of the blackboard he wrote down some text references and on the opposite side he wrote down a list – bird, flower, tree, name of girl, name of town etc. They were to find out the links. A boy aged nine came to his desk after a while and said he had got all the answers except one. 'You see, I don't know whether adultery is a flower or not.' The mischievous chaplain said, 'I think you'd better go and ask Mrs Urch that one.' Which he promptly did! Collapse of Head Teacher!

## August 31st

When the astronauts on Discovery 5 Space Mission came to describe their journey, they said:

'The first day or so we all pointed to our countries. The third or fourth day we were pointing to our continents. But the fifth day we were aware of only one earth.'

JEWISH PRAYER FOR INTERNATIONAL UNDERSTANDING

Lord of peace, be with those who guide the destinies of the world so that an end may come to boasting and vainglory, and the reign of arrogance dwindle in our time. Give them the courage to speak the truth and the humility to listen. Help us all to put the good of our fellowmen above our own ambitions, and the truth which does not profit us above the lie which does. So may we stand upright, freed from the burden of fear and the weight of suspicion, learning to trust each other.

Help each one of us to bring his own offer of understanding, and his own sacrifice for peace, so that we are at peace with ourselves and live in peace with those around us. Then in tranquillity may we all go forward to build your kingdom in the world until the earth shall be filled with your knowledge as the waters cover the sea.

# SEPTEMBER

*Earth is here so kind,*
*that just tickle her with a hoe*
*and she laughs with a harvest.*  *Douglas Jerrold*

**September 1st**
Leslie Pickney Hill was a Negro poet who wrote the following
poem which has been, whether in or out of the classroom, my
constant inspiration. For we are all teaching somebody or other
all the days of our life, and mostly we are not conscious of what
knowledge, good or ill we are transmitting. Hermione Hill
Logan, Leslie Pickney Hill's daughter, has given her permission for its use.

### THE TEACHER

Lord, who am I to teach the way
To little children day by day
So prone myself to go astray?

I teach them Knowledge, but I know
How faint they flicker and how low
The candles of my knowledge grow.

I teach them Power to will and do,
But only now to learn anew
My own great weakness through and through.

I teach them Love for all mankind
And all God's creatures, but I find
My love comes lagging far behind.

Lord, if their guide I still must be,
Oh, let the little children see
The teacher leaning hard on thee.

**September 2nd**
It all depends on me, a nobody,
If nobody I can and dare to be,
Effaced of self, dependent on the All
Invulnerable, though heavens fall.  *Anon.*

97

## September 3rd
Every child comes into the world with the message that God
does not yet despair of man. *Rabindranath Tagore*

## September 4th
A French priest, Père Duval, said that he learnt more from the
hands of his father and the lips of his mother than from any
catechism. He said that from their way of life he reckoned that
God must be a person very close to us, to whom it is very pleas-
ant to speak when one's work is done. He looked at his father
kneeling on the kitchen floor, and he thought: 'My father, who
is so strong, who is head of our house, who can drive the oxen,
who doesn't kow-tow to the mayor, or to the rich people, or to
any ruffians . . . my father, when he is in the presence of God,
is just like a child.'

And when he looked at his mother, he said, 'God must be a
very homely person if one talks to him with a child in one's
arms, or with an apron on. And he must be a very important
person if, when Mother speaks to him, she does not pay any
attention to either the cat or the storm outside.'

## September 5th
When I was very young, my father had a train accident which
meant a leg amputation. I do not remember it happening,
though I remember sitting on the cage over his legs when I saw
him in his hospital bed. Later, I was told by the colleague who
had accompanied him to hospital that in Casualty when they
were trying to cut off his clothing, he said, 'Be sure to tell my
wife that I am having a really ripping time!'

## September 6th
If any man offend not in word, the same is a perfect man, and
able also to bridle the whole body. Behold, we put bits in the
horses' mouths, that they may obey us; and we turn about their
whole body. Behold also the ships, which though they be so
great, and are driven of fierce winds, yet are they turned about
with a very small helm, whithersoever the governor listeth.
Even so the tongue is a little member, and boasteth great
things. Behold, how great a matter a little fire kindleth!
*James 3:2–6 (AV)*

## September 7th

Set our feet on lofty places,
Gird our lives that they may be
Armoured with all Christlike graces
In the fight to set men free.
Grant us wisdom, grant us courage
That we fail not man nor thee.

*Harry Emerson Fosdick*

## September 8th

One day I was amusing myself and a group of children with a magnet, a sewing needle, a dead match and a bowl of water. After rubbing the needle up and down on the magnet, we stuck it through the centre of the match. 'Now float it on the water,' I said. No matter how often we tried it, after the needle had swung round for a while, it always settled at North. They were all duly impressed, until I hid the magnet in my clasped hand and waved it over the needle. Consternation followed as the needle went out of control. I had caused the experiment to collapse by a wave of the hand.

The magnet, which had given direction to the needle in the first instance, had also the power to make it go wild.

That's a sobering thought as we realise what consciously or unconsciously we rub off on to others.

## September 9th

Precocious child, when asked what age he was: 'Do you mean my mental age, my reading age, or my chronological age?'

## September 10th

### WHEN I GROW OLD

You can't be very happy when you're young.
You have to go downstairs and walk among
Uncles and aunts, shake hands and say, 'Goodnight'
As you are told.
But I shan't wash my neck, nor be polite
Nor try to laugh when Uncle Joseph talks
Nor have that tired feeling after walks
When I grow old.                    *Unattributed*

### September 11th

Graham Greene, the writer, once told a fellow writer that he envied him. 'You see, you are happy – unless you have a special reason for being unhappy. You like people – unless you have a special reason to dislike them. I am the opposite. I am always unhappy, unless I have a good reason to be happy. And I dislike people unless I have a very good reason to like them.' I find that immensely sad, though I fear there are many in our stricken world who have the same sentiments.

### September 12th

A teacher, after telling her pupils the story of the Good Samaritan, asked them what they could learn from the story. One pupil said, 'If I am ever in any kind of trouble, people should always come and help me.' Though maybe that child was expressing what we often think but do not dare say, I guess the teacher would have to tell the story all over again with its important opening question as to who is our neighbour, and Christ's command following, 'Go and do likewise.' We can so easily get by in life, if we only compare ourselves with one another, instead of placing ourselves alongside the Christ.

### September 13th

When you do some act of charity, do not announce it with a flourish of trumpets, as the hypocrites do in synagogue and in the streets to win admiration from men. I tell you this: they have their reward already. No; when you do some act of charity, do not let your left hand know what your right is doing; your good deed must be in secret, and your Father who sees what is done in secret will reward you.     *Matthew 6:2–4 (NEB)*

### September 14th

A GAELIC PRAYER FOR TIMES OF DISSATISFACTION

Often I wish I were other than I am.
I get weary of the sombre tide
of the little fields
of this brooding isle.

I long to be rid of the burden of my duty
  and to take part in a fuller life.

O God, you who are wisdom and pity both,
  set me free from the tyranny of desire.

Help me to find my joy
  in my acceptance of what is my purpose;
    in the eyes of friends
    in work well done
      in serenity born of trust
        and, most of all,
    in the awareness of your presence
        within my spirit.

## September 15th

Rossini wrote his opera *Moses in Egypt* especially to be performed during Lent. But he had forgotten that the stage hands in the St Carlo Opera House had not had any divine revelation about how to achieve the parting of the Red Sea. Their efforts were a complete disaster and met with such criticism that Rossini had to try to redeem the situation. The result was his writing of what has become one of the best-loved pieces – Moses' Prayer. It is quite a simple tune, but poignant and haunting. Moses and the Children of Israel sing it praying for pity on their plight. Then it is taken up by Aaron, asking God, who can command the elements, to guide the uncertain feet of his children. Next Miriam and her daughter take up the tune and pray for sweet peace for grieving hearts. When Moses' Prayer was first sung in public, the previous inadequacies became quite obliterated.

Rossini died in Paris, but his body was reburied in Florence twenty years after his death. Moses' Prayer was sung as a tribute to him at the funeral service. I wonder has there ever been another funeral service at which the congregation called for an encore – for that is what happened.

Talk about turning our stumbling blocks into stepping-stones!

## September 16th

There are essentially four kinds of risk:
The risk one must accept.
The risk one can afford to take.
The risk one cannot afford to take.
The risk one cannot afford not to take.           *P. F. Drucker*

## September 17th

> I held it truth, with him who sings
> To one clear harp in divers tones,
> That men may rise on stepping stones
> Of their dead selves to higher things.
> > *Tennyson:* In Memoriam

## September 18th

A different kind of opera mishap took place in Dublin, when
Gounod's *Faust* was being staged and Mephistopheles had to
descend to the nether regions by a trap door on the stage with
mock flames surrounding it. The set designers had reckoned
without the enormous bulk of the male opera singer and he
became wedged halfway through the trap door. Never lost for
a witty retort, an Irishman rescued the occasion, at least for the
audience, by bellowing out across the auditorium, 'Thank God!
Hell's full at last!'

## September 19th

Wise madness is better than foolish sanity.
> *Cervantes:* Don Quixote

## September 20th

Who is a wise man and endued with knowledge among you?
Let him show out of a good conversation his works with meekness of wisdom. But if you have bitter envying and strife in
your hearts, glory not, and lie not against the truth. This
wisdom descendeth not from above, but is earthly, sensual,
devilish. For where envying and strife is, there is confusion and
every evil work. But the wisdom that is from above is first pure,
then peaceable, gentle, and easy to be intreated, full of mercy
and good fruits, without partiality, and without hypocrisy. And
the fruit of righteousness is sown in peace of them that make
peace.                          *James 3:13–18 (AV)*

**September 21st**

Do not forget us, O Lord,
As we forget you amidst our daily cares,
See how busy and serious we become
About our important lives!
Help us to accept your gift now:
a moment of time
to smile and give thanks.

Look graciously on those
who know no rest, no joy.
May we be sisters and brothers in Christ
and together come into his freedom.

*Michael Urch*

**September 22nd**

It seemed most extraordinary to me a few years ago that one of the pieces of music which featured for several weeks on *Top of the Pops* was a very beautiful, but very sombre, prayer which had been written on wall 3 of Cell 3 in the basement of a building called 'The Palace' in Zakopane in Poland. This was the headquarters of the Gestapo and in that cell had been imprisoned on 26th September 1944 a girl, eighteen years old, called Helena Wanda Blazusiakowna. She wrote 'the imprisoned prayer', as Gorecki, who set it to music in the Third Symphony, called it. It was hauntingly beautiful, and I found a story associated with it which is also hauntingly beautiful.

On the fiftieth anniversary of Hitler's attack on Poland (which caused the outbreak of World War 2) there were memorial events and music in various cities including Brunswick's St Magnus Church which had been rebuilt after its destruction towards the end of the war. The congregation had met in a spirit of repentance and reconciliation, and just before the soprano solo voice singing the Gestapo Prison prayer, the lights were lowered and later extinguished. Then, when all the music had silenced, a previously hidden stained glass window was floodlit from the darkness outside, and the silent congregation saw, as the bells pealed out, the picture of the Israelites fleeing from their captors as the Red Sea parted.

And that is the story accompanying the prayer which became

Top of the Pops in Britain a few years later. We must not isolate the music which moves us from the realities of all that gave it birth.

## September 23rd
A Yugoslav poet who won a Nobel prize wrote: 'Only the ignorant and unwise could hold that the past is dead and forever separated by an impenetrable wall from the present.'

## September 24th
Amos Oz, a well-known Israeli novelist, went with Professor Hisham Sharaki, one of the authors of the PLO Constitution, to visit some places they dared not go on their own. Together they wanted to investigate the attempts at Israeli/Palestinian reconciliation.

Oz stood on the edge of a former battlefield, and said, 'Next to losing a battle, the most terrible thing is winning it.'

## September 25th
> In war: resolution
> In defeat: defiance
> In victory: magnanimity
> In peace: goodwill          *Winston Churchill*

## September 26th
It was during those long and lonely years that my hunger for the freedom of my own people became a hunger for the freedom of all people, white and black. I knew as well as I knew anything that the oppressor must be liberated as well as the oppressed. A man who takes away another man's freedom is a prisoner of hatred; he is locked behind the bars of prejudice and narrow-mindedness. I am not truly free if I am taking away someone else's freedom, just as surely as I am not free when my freedom is taken from me. The oppressed and the oppressor alike are robbed of their humanity.

*Nelson Mandela, in* Long Walk to Freedom

## September 27th
Love your enemies, do good to them which hate you, bless them that curse you, and pray for them which despitefully use you. And unto him that smiteth thee on the one cheek offer

also the other; and him that taketh away thy cloke forbid not to take thy coat also. . . . For if ye love them which love you, what thank have ye? for sinners also love those that love them. And if ye do good to them which do good to you, what thank have ye? for sinners also do even the same. And if ye lend to them of whom ye hope to receive, what thank have ye? for sinners also lend to sinners, to receive as much again. But love ye your enemies, and do good and lend, hoping for nothing again; and your reward shall be great, and ye shall be the children of the Highest: for he is kind unto the unthankful and to the evil. Be ye therefore merciful, as your Father also is merciful.

*Luke 6:27–29, 32–36 (AV)*

### September 28th

Richard of Chichester was Bishop there in the thirteenth century and fought for integrity in the church. He was strict with himself and his diocese and was constantly on the side of the poor, fighting those who oppressed them or tried to take precedence over them. His prayer is a much used and beloved one.

> Thanks to you, my Lord Jesus Christ
> for all the gifts you have won for me,
> For all the pains and insults
> You have borne for me.
> O merciful Redeemer
> Friend and brother,
> May I know you more clearly,
> Love you more dearly,
> And follow you more nearly,
> For ever and ever. Amen.

### September 29th

An ecumenical meeting was being held in a hall when the fire alarm went off. The Roman Catholics consulted, and decided to light a few candles. The Episcopalians started discussing in what order they should emerge from the exit. The Baptists started a prayer meeting. The Methodists discussed what Wesleyan hymn was appropriate for the occasion and the Church of Scotland decided to form yet another committee that would be equipped to discuss the emergency.

## September 30th

As we come to the end of another month, I have been pondering the name September, and how our ninth month has a name which means seventh month. It is because the calendars of old started the new year in March. The old Dutch name for September was Autumn month, whilst the old Saxon was Barley month. In the old French calendar it was Fruit month. There is even a September Bible, so called because it was published at Wittenberg in September, 1522. It was actually Luther's German translation of the New Testament.

# OCTOBER

*No Spring, nor Summer beauty hath such grace*
*As I have seen on one Autumnal face.*        *John Donne*

## October 1st

Sometimes a new adaptation of Scripture helps to light up its meaning and extend its solace. Ian Pitt-Watson's adaptation of Psalm 139 never ceases to move and succour me.

> Thou art before me, Lord, Thou art behind,
> And Thou above me hast spread out Thy hand,
> Such knowledge is too wonderful for me,
> Too high to grasp, too great to understand.
>
> Then whither from Thy Spirit shall I go
> And whither from Thy presence shall I flee?
> If I ascend to heaven Thou art there
> And in the lowest depths I meet with Thee.
>
> If I should take my flight into the dawn,
> If I should dwell on ocean's farthest shore,
> Thy mighty hand would rest upon me still
> And Thy right hand would guard me evermore.
>
> If I should say, 'Darkness will cover me,
> And I shall hide within the veil of night',
> Surely the darkness is not dark to Thee;
> The night is as the day, the darkness light.
>
> Search me, O God, search me and know my heart,
> Try me, O God, my mind and spirit try;
> Keep me from any path that gives Thee pain
> And lead me in the everlasting way.

## October 2nd

It is extraordinarily difficult at times to know how to direct our minds and attitudes and behaviour. It may help to ask ourselves some straightforward questions.

What is this action, this attitude of mine doing to the other person?

Does this attitude, this action of mine add to suffering, or does it lessen it?

What is this attitude, this action of mine doing to myself?

What does this attitude, this action of mine do to my relationship with God?

## October 3rd

Cardinal Hume has said that one can be more touched by contact with holy people than by any number of sermons.

When my husband died, still a young man, his congregation did not say that he had preached many a good sermon, though he had. The memorial they gave him was, 'He was a good man.'

> For me, 'twas not the truth you taught
> To you so clear, to me so dim
> But when you came to me
> You brought a sense of Him.
>
> And from your eyes He beckons me,
> And from your lips His love is shed,
> Till I lose sight of you
> And see the Christ instead.                    *Unattributed*

## October 4th

Christy Nolan won the Whitbread Book of the Year award in 1987 for his book *Under the Eye of the Clock*. He has cerebral palsy and has never been able to convey his meaning in ordinary speech. But he commends those who helped to decipher the code of his facial expressions, his eye movements and his body language. Through the character of Joseph in his semi-autobiographical writing, he said that it was at such moments that he recognised the face of God in human form. It glimmered in their kindness to him, it glowed in their keenness, it hinted in their caring, indeed it caressed in their gaze.

Yet without bitterness he reveals not long after how someone blessed with normality and reputed to be Christian had so schooled himself in the art of saying 'No' that you knew he would always, always veto any attempts to educate those with special needs.

**October 5th**

The Bard of Tyrone, Rev. W. F. Marshall, died just a few days before my husband. His Te Deum was 'Thank God for a good breakfast . . . and the prospect of a good day's fishing.' Someone who enjoyed his ministry said, 'If you fish as well as you preach – well, God help the fish!'

**October 6th**

Put on therefore, as the elect of God, holy and beloved, bowels of mercies, kindness, humbleness of mind, meekness, long-suffering; forbearing one another, and forgiving one another, if any man have a quarrel against any; even as Christ forgave you, so also do ye. And above all these things put on charity, which is the bond of perfectness. And let the peace of God rule in your hearts, to the which also ye are called in one body; and be ye thankful. . . . And whatsoever ye do in word or deed, do all in the name of the Lord Jesus, giving thanks to God and the Father by him. *Colossians 3:12–15, 17 (AV)*

**October 7th**

A FIFTH-CENTURY PRAYER

O God, you in your lovingkindness do both begin and finish all good things. Grant that as we glory in the beginning of your grace, so we may rejoice in its completion. Through Jesus Christ our Lord.

**October 8th**

There is a well-meaning attitude in our churches today about giving money for the Third World at harvest time, *instead* of decorating the church with harvest gifts. I wish that the one way of marking harvest did not exclude the other, for in Exodus 23:19 a good principle was adopted in ordering that the first of the first-fruits of the land should be brought to the House of God. Some folk say the first Harvest Festival in British churches dates back to a service inaugurated in 1843 by a vicar in Cornwall, but Harvest Home ceremonies were earlier than that.

The church mouse of Sir John Betjeman would be hard-pressed in some of our churches today at Harvest Thanksgiving.

Here among long-discarded cassocks,
Damp stools and half-split-open hassocks
Here where the vicar never looks
I nibble through old service books.
Lean and alone I spend my days
Behind this Church of England baize.
I share my half-forgotten room
With two oil lamps and half a broom.
The cleaner never bothers me
So here I eat my frugal tea.
My bread is saw-dust mixed with straw;
My jam is polish for the floor.
Christmas and Easter may be feasts
For congregations and for priests.
And so may Whitsun. All the same,
They do not fill my meagre frame.

For me the only feast at all
Is Autumn's Harvest Festival,
When I can satisfy my want
With ears of corn around the font.
I climb the eagle's brazen head
To burrow through a loaf of bread.
I scramble up the pulpit stair
And gnaw the marrows hanging there.
It is enjoyable to taste
These items ere they go to waste;
But how annoying when one finds
That other mice with pagan minds
Come into church my food to share
Who have no proper business there.
Two field mice who have no desire
To be baptized, invade the choir.
A large and most unfriendly rat
Comes in to see what we are at.
He says he thinks there is no God
And yet he comes . . . it's rather odd.
This year he stole a sheaf of wheat
(It screened our special preacher's seat),
And prosperous mice from far away

Came in to hear the organ play,
And under cover of the notes
Ate through the altar's sheaf of oats.
A Low Church mouse who thinks that I
Am too papistical and High,
Yet somehow doesn't think it wrong
To munch through Harvest Evensong,
While I, who starve the whole year through,
Must share my food with rodents who
Except at this time of the year
Not once inside the church appear.
Within the human world, I know
Such goings-on could not be so,
For human beings only do
What their religion tells them to.

They read the Bible every day
And always, night and morning, pray,
And just like me, the good church mouse,
Worship each week in God's own house,
But all the same, it's strange to me
How very full the church can be
With people I don't see at all
Except at Harvest Festival.

## October 9th

The pupils of my rural school in the Queen's Silver Jubilee
Year had imaginative ideas for raising money for The Prince's
Trust which was to help young people help others. The
youngest in the school were growing beans and getting parents
and relations to sponsor them, by the centimetre of growth.
When the Prince arrived by helicopter at the town nearby, a
few of the pupils were asked to meet him, because of their
efforts. As we were about to depart, Kenneth, who had raised
the most money because his bean was the longest, insisted on
taking the bean, complete with its plastic cup, to show to the
Prince. It was a very hot day, and the bean continued to wilt
until the Prince, on his arrival, said, 'I'm afraid your bean is
now a bit of a has-been!' Kenneth achieved instant fame, as the
Lord Lieutenant who accompanied the Prince told the story in
public on a number of occasions.

**October 10th**

Even after a bad harvest, there must be sowing.

*Seneca, in a first-century letter*

**October 11th**

Your days on earth are just so few
That there's exactly time to do
The things that don't appeal to you.   *Unattributed*

**October 12th**

God asks not for success
But faithfulness,
Not for great skill
But that we do his will.   *Author unknown*

**October 13th**

NATIONAL THANKSGIVING

Answer us with deeds not words,
    with terror and victory
  O God, who rescued us! –
hope of remotest peoples
    and far-away islands!

You build up the mountain ranges
    in Your great strength;
You calm the stormy seas
    and the wild waves;
    sea monsters cower
    at Your wonders;
You make dawn and sunset
    sing aloud for joy.
You come and water the earth,
    its richness is Your gift:
mighty rivers flow full with rain
    making the earth ready for sowing;
in wet furrows, pressed sods,
    softened with steady showers
You bless the growing grain.
You bless the year with Your bounty –
    wagon tracks drip with blessings.

The wild moors shout,
   the hills gird themselves
   with happiness and joy.
Sheep clothe the hills like a cloak,
   the valleys are dressed with corn,
   shouting and singing for joy!
*Alan Dale's rendering of Psalm 65:5–12*

## October 14th

Lord, you have kept your promise that as long as mankind remains, seedtime and harvest will not fail. Yet your bounty is not matched by open-handedness on our part. We give grudgingly and often only what we have left over. You have given us the resources and the power to help save our world from starvation and disease. You are willing to give us also the love, the strength, the determination and the wisdom to be good stewards. Help us to seek all your gifts, so that your bounty may be matched by our greatness of heart. For Christ's sake.

## October 15th

Near where I live is the former home of an esteemed Scottish poet, William Soutar. In 1938 he wrote: 'Silence is perhaps the greatest Hallelujah'. Strange words, because he had been confined to what he called his 'Quiet Room' for seven and a half years. He could have been forgiven for deploring his solitariness and his long-drawn-out illness. But Soutar did not leave it there. He goes on to say that silence is not enough. 'Every day is life's Messiah,' he wrote, 'and joy needs to be met and shared.'

Sometimes we are frightened of silence, maybe because we have known too much of the negative kind – loneliness; the chilling silence of disapproval or antagonism; being ignored or shut out. But we are blessed indeed if we know the rich and comfortable silences with friends and lovers when words are not needed to communicate; when speech would be an intrusion into a precious time of worship.

What about those times when we have kept silent, when to have spoken would have righted a wrong? Or when we uttered a harsh and cruel judgment when silence would have been the better choice?

The writer in Ecclesiastes knew well that there is a time to be silent and a time to speak.

## October 16th

There are some people who have no option but to live in a silent world. I am always very moved when I see a deaf choir, *signing* rather than *singing* hymns. The first time I ever saw this poetry in motion was when Richard Dimbleby introduced some small deaf Korean orphans signing Away in a Manger. Since then I have felt unbearably moved when I have watched other deaf choirs. The sign for Jesus Christ is to point to the 'nail-prints' in the palm of the hand. The sign for forgiveness is taking a finger and 'wiping the slate clean'.

## October 17th

SONGS OF PRAISE FOR THE DEAF

Let them praise the Lord
    in silence
with hands that have an openness
denied to shamming tongues.

See them describe the deaf air
with the jerky span of butterflies
movements of inevitable life:
the evolution of roses
the silent sway of corn.

See them draw Galilee's quiet shores
evoke the mystery of Golgotha's dark vale;
see their hands knit words
as they praise the differing movements
    of creatures great and small.

Listen to the gravity of their praise
echoing through the stillness
    of ancient valleys
and nature's first formations
devoid of tawdry human sound.
Listen to them praise
the resonant silence
    of all creation.

*Tom Pow*

## October 18th

My son told me once that he was going to an international retreat where they were going 'to learn to be silent in seven languages'.

## October 19th

A Dublin woman asked her husband had he any ideas about how they would celebrate their Silver Wedding.

'Yes,' he replied. 'With three minutes' silence!'

## October 20th

Be not rash with thy mouth, and let not thine heart be hasty to utter any thing before God: for God is in heaven, and thou upon the earth: therefore let thy words be few.

*Ecclesiastes 5:2 (AV)*

## October 21st

PRAYER FROM JAPAN

O make my heart so still, so still,
When I am deep in prayer
That I might hear the white mist-wreaths
Losing themselves in air.

## October 22nd

Some years back, I was in Helsinki and had to travel daily across the city to my son's flat. I marvelled at the strong, silent Finns who rarely seemed to communicate on transport. On arrival at the flat, my daughter-in-law gave me to read a very commendable essay she had written in English, to be given to an International Women's Conference later. It was about Jesus' conversation with the woman at the well in Samaria. When I handed it back to her, I said wryly to her, 'If Jesus had been in Finland instead, he would have had some difficulty getting any kind of conversation going at all.'

Next day, as I sat on the tram making the same journey, a man got on and spoke to me in Finnish. I explained that I did not know Finnish, so in perfect English he asked me to give him warning when we were one stop ahead of the Post Office. He then engaged me in conversation all the way to his destination. On leaving, he shook my hand and said, 'When you meet your family today, tell them that you, a complete stranger, helped a Finn who was born in Helsinki and has lived all his life here to find his way. You see I am now almost totally blind.' I was duly chastened.

## October 23rd
I was talking recently to a man who had lost his sight ten years ago. Philosophically he told me how he had had to adapt to many changes in his life. And then gleefully he said, 'But there's one part of my sight that's even better than it was before – and that's my hindsight.'

## October 24th
Sir John Fielding, who lived in the eighteenth century, was well known as the Blind Magistrate. He was reputed to know count-less thieves by their voices.

## October 25th
Vision is the art of seeing things invisible.                 *Jonathan Swift*

## October 26th
> O, wad some Power the giftie gie us
> To see oursels as ithers see us.
> It wad frae monie a blunder free us
> An' foolish notion.        *Robert Burns: 'To A Louse'*

## October 27th
This then is the message which we have heard of him, and declare unto you, that God is light, and in him is no darkness at all. If we say that we have fellowship with him, and walk in darkness, we lie, and do not the truth: but if we walk in the light, as he is in the light, we have fellowship one with another, and the blood of Jesus Christ his Son cleanseth us from all sin.
*1 John 1:5–7 (AV)*

## October 28th
John Henry Newman, who wrote the well-known hymn 'Lead Kindly Light', gives us the following prayer, which echoes some of the emotions of that much-loved hymn:

O Lord, I give myself to you. I trust you wholly. You are wiser than I – more loving to me than I am myself. Deign to fulfil your high purposes in me whatever they may be. Work in and through me. I am born to serve you, to be yours, to be your instrument. Let me be your blind instrument. I ask not to see. I ask not to know. I ask simply to be used.

### October 29th
One of our faithful baby-sitters told us one night that she had tried to encourage one of our very tiny young daughters to drink up her bedtime milk by telling her that she wouldn't grow up to be a pretty lady if she didn't. She took a sip, and then after a long hard look at her carer, she asked very sympathetically, 'Did you not drink up your milk when you were a little girl?'

### October 30th
Lord Louis Mountbatten once said that his wife described an expert as 'X – an unknown quantity; and spurt, a drip under pressure!'

### October 31st
I asked for knowledge – power to control things;
I was granted understanding – to learn to love persons.
I asked for strength to become a Great Man;
I was made weak to become a better Man.
I asked for wealth to make friends;
I became poor to keep friends.
I asked for all things to enjoy life;
I was granted all life to enjoy things.
I cried for Pity. I was offered Sympathy.
I craved for healing of my own disorders;
I received insight into another's suffering.
I prayed to God for safety – to tread the trodden path;
I was granted danger, to lose track, and find the Way.
I got nothing that I prayed for;
I am among all men richly blessed.           *Anon.*

# NOVEMBER

*For man, Autumn is a time of harvest and gathering together:*
*For nature, it is a time of sowing, of scattering abroad.*

*Edwin Way Teale*

**November 1st**

If you have ever had a period of sleepless nights, perhaps through the care of a sick child, or watching with someone in pain or distress, you may appreciate this Jewish prayer:

Lord, let your light be only for the day,
And the darkness for the night.
And let my dress, my poor humble dress
Lie quietly over my chair at night.

Let the church bells be silent,
My neighbour Ivan not ring them at night.
Let the wind not waken the children
Out of their sleep at night.

Let the hen sleep on its roost, the horse in the stable,
All through the night.
Remove the stone from the middle of the road
That the thief may not stumble at night.

Let heaven be quiet during the night.
Restrain the lightning, silence the thunder.
They should not frighten mothers giving birth
To their babies at night.

And me too protect against fire and water,
Protect my poor roof at night.
Let my dress, my poor humble dress
Lie quietly over my chair at night.          *Nachum Bonze*

**November 2nd**

A child kept calling downstairs repeatedly when she should have been asleep. In the end the mother, not caring that she was not being politically correct, said, 'If I hear your voice once more, I'll come up and give you a smacked bottom.'

There was quietness for a brief period, and then a wistful little voice: 'Mummy, when you come up to give me a smacked bottom, will you please bring me a drink of water?'

## November 3rd
The following words have been attributed to Churchill, but he denied ever having written them:

> The gates of Fame are open wide,
> Its halls are always full,
> And some go in by the door called PUSH
> And some by the door called PULL.

## November 4th
Two things a genuine Christian never does. He never makes light of any known sin, and he never admits it to be invincible.

*Canon Liddon*

## November 5th
I never wonder to see men wicked. But I often wonder to see them not ashamed.

*Dean Swift*

## November 6th
Consider the lilies of the field, how they grow; they toil not, neither do they spin: And yet I say unto you, That even Solomon in all his glory was not arrayed like one of these. Wherefore, if God so clothe the grass of the field, which to day is, and to morrow is cast into the oven, shall he not much more clothe you, O ye of little faith? Therefore take no thought, saying, What shall we eat? or, What shall we drink? or, Wherewithal shall we be clothed? (For after all these things do the Gentiles seek:) for your heavenly Father knoweth that ye have need of all these things. But seek ye first the kingdom of God, and his righteousness; and all these things shall be added unto you. Take therefore no thought for the morrow: for the morrow shall take thought for the things of itself. Sufficient unto the day is the evil thereof.

*Matthew 6:28–34 (AV)*

## November 7th

Here is a blessing adapted from one attributed to Charles I:

### CLOSE YOUR EYES

Close your eyes and rest secure;
Your soul is safe, your body sure.
He who guards you, he who keeps,
Never slumbers, never sleeps.

A quiet conscience in the breast
Has only peace, has only rest.
The music and the mirth of kings
Are out of tune till conscience sings.

So close your eyes in peace and rest secure;
No sleep so sweet as yours; no rest so sure.

## November 8th

### A COMMUNION DRAMA

My son Michael tells of an experimental service which was held when celebrating communion. A group had been asked to take the story of Jesus healing the paralysed man and to use it in some way to enlighten the congregation about the sacrament they were about to share. After the reading of the Gospel passage, one of the group came forward to the front of the table, representing Jesus. Suddenly the main doors of the church opened and four companions entered, carrying their friend. They laid him at the feet of Jesus, saying, 'This is our friend who is paralysed.' Jesus raised him up, embraced him and said, 'You are free. Go in peace.'

The freed person jumped with joy and ran to someone in the congregation. Bringing her forward to Jesus, he said, 'This is my friend who is paralysed with anxiety.' Jesus embraced her and set her free. She, in turn, brought someone forward, saying, 'This is my friend who is paralysed with wealth.' After the embrace and words of freedom, he in turn brought someone paralysed by poverty. Next came one paralysed by racial prejudice, and so it was possible to develop the theme indefinitely.

The minister of the congregation where 'the freedom of those that were bound' was acted out faced the congregation before the bread and wine were shared. Because the very nature of Christ's presence at the sacrament had been demonstrated, he said, 'If you are paralysed, do you have a friend you can rely on to bring you to Jesus? If you have a friend who is paralysed, have you the courage and faith to get together with others and bring your friend to Jesus? Let us bear each other's burdens and share each other's joys and sorrows.'

## November 9th

I love you, not only for what you are, but for what I am when I am with you.

I love you, not only for what you have made of yourself, but for what you are making of me.

I love you for putting your hand into my heaped-up heart and passing over all the weak and foolish things that you can't help dimly seeing there. And for drawing out into the light all the beautiful radiant belongings that no one else had looked far enough to see.

I love you for ignoring the possibilities of the fool and weakling in me and for adding to the music in me by worshipful listening.

I love you because you are helping me to make of the lumber of my life, not a tavern but a temple, and of the works of my every day, not a reproach, but a song.

I love you because you have done more for me than any creed could have done to make me good, and more than any fate could have done to make me happy.

You have done it, without a touch, without a word, without a sign.

You have done it by just being yourself.

Perhaps that is what being a friend means after all.

*Unattributed*

## November 10th

One colleague to another as the boss approached:

'Here comes a self-made man!'

'Well he certainly must have saved God a lot of trouble!'

## November 11th

This is Remembrance Day. When I was in New Zealand some years back I came on the following poem entitled 'I Am Not There' and it was attributed to a young New Zealand Rugby player, Steven Day, who had died of cancer. The next time I heard of it was some years later when a young soldier called Stephen Cummins died in an IRA explosion in Londonderry. He had sent the poem to his family. It was to be used later in a memorial window and after establishing that Stephen was not the poet himself, a search was made as to its writer. Some say it is a Navaho Burial Prayer, others attribute it to American immigrants, but there is no certainty now as to its origin.

### I AM NOT THERE

Do not stand at my grave and weep
I am not there, I do not sleep.
I am a thousand winds that blow
I am the diamond, glimpsed on snow
I am the sunlight on ripened grain
I am the gentle autumn rain.
When you awake in the morning hush
I am the swift uplifting rush
Of quiet birds in circled flight.
I am the soft stars that shine at night.
Do not stand at my grave and cry;
I am not there. I did not die.

## November 12th

Suffering passes; having suffered never passes.    *Jean Péguy*

### WASTE

Waste of Muscle, waste of Brain,
Waste of Patience, waste of Pain,
Waste of Manhood, waste of Health,
Waste of Beauty, waste of Wealth,
Waste of Blood and waste of Tears,
Waste of Youth's most precious years,
Waste of ways the saints have trod,
Waste of Glory, waste of God –
        WAR!

*G. A. Studdert-Kennedy*

### November 13th

Jesus said unto her [Martha], I am the resurrection, and the life: he that believeth in me, though he were dead, yet shall he live: and whosoever liveth and believeth in me shall never die. Believest thou this?                    *John 11:25–26 (AV)*

### November 14th

This prayer was written by Bishop Brent in the First World War:

We give them back to you, dear Lord, who gave them to us. Yet as you did not lose them in giving, so we have not lost them by their return. Not as the world gives, do you give, O Lover of souls. What you gave, you do not take away; for what is yours is ours also if we are yours. And life is eternal, and Love is immortal, and Death is only a horizon and a horizon is nothing save the limit of our sight.

Lift us up, strong Son of God, that we may see further; cleanse our eyes that we may see more clearly; draw us closer to yourself that we may know ourselves to be nearer to our loved ones who are with you. And while you prepare a place for us, prepare us also for that happy place, that where they are and you are, we too may be for evermore.

### November 15th

After I retired, I showed a friend a tapestry I intended to start work on. 'How long will it take?' she asked.

'It will take as long as it will take,' I answered, being still caught up in the euphoria of no deadlines to meet, no bells or timetable to obey – just as someone in my native Ireland has said, 'When God made time here, he made plenty of it and to spare.'

So I was somewhat chastened a few weeks later when after whirling around in frenetic activity for a whole morning and getting nowhere fast, I sank into a chair, saying to myself, 'I am late for my appointment with me!'

These are the words of a young Russian poet, Mayakovsky, from a poem about a young boy who had lost his true self in a big and complicated world.

When Jesus turned away from the crowd and sought solitude in communion with his Father, it wasn't a selfish turning away, but a necessary space to recover from spiritual exhaustion. He knew too well what it meant when virtue had gone out of him. If sometimes we have to say we are late for an appointment with ourselves, it's time we made an urgent appointment with our God.

### November 16th
Boy to Dad: Dad, can I ask you a question?
Dad (with head buried in newspaper): Not now!
Boy: Dad, I want to ask you a question.
Dad: NOT NOW!
Boy (after a long silence, and then rather wistfully): Dad, is there something wrong with having to ask a question?
Dad: Why no, son! If you don't ask, you'll never learn!

### November 17th

> If you dig a hole
> You may find coal
> But mostly you get
> Just mud and wet!
> *John o' the North (H. T. Browne)*

### November 18th
One of my colleagues who had been off ill told me that on her return she proceeded to play (as she was only ever able to do) the Assembly hymn tune with right hand alone. One very young girl stopped her in her tracks and said, 'Miss H. who was here when you were ill played us that tune. But she wasn't as clever as you, for she needed both hands.'

### November 19th
If you must grouse about the weather, do it poetically like Thomas Hood:

NOVEMBER

> No sun, no moon,
> No morn, no noon,
> No dawn, no dusk, no proper time of day;
> No sky, no earthly view,
> No distance looking blue. . . .

No warmth, no cheerfulness, no healthful ease,
No comfortable feel in any member,
No shade, no shine, no butterflies, no bees,
No fruit, no flowers, no leaves, no trees;
November!

## November 20th

The word which came to Jeremiah from the LORD, saying,
Arise, and go down to the potter's house, and there I will cause
thee to hear my words. Then I went down to the potter's house,
and behold, he wrought a work on the wheels. And the vessel
that he made of clay was marred in the hand of the potter: so
he made it again another vessel, as seemed good to the potter
to make it. Then the word of the LORD came to me, saying, O
house of Israel, cannot I do with you as this potter? saith the
LORD. Behold, as the clay is in the potter's hand, so are ye in my
hand, O house of Israel.                    *Jeremiah 18:1–6 (AV)*

## November 21st

This is an adaptation of an old prayer by Thomas a Kempis
(1379–1471):

O Lord, you know what is best for me, let this or that be done,
as you shall please. Give what you will, and how much you will
and when you will. Deal with me in whatever way you think
best, and as it pleases you. Place me wherever you will, and use
me in everything just as you want to. Here I am, waiting to be
your servant, prepared for what you have for me. For I do not
wish to live for myself, but for you. Oh, that I might do that,
worthily and perfectly.

## November 22nd

When I was a young student the fashionable phrase to use was
'I couldn't care less.' At the time someone told me the true story
of a wise parish priest in France in the nineteenth century. He
was beloved by those to whom he constantly gave wise counsel.
Two young disreputable youths passed his house one night,
and as they cared neither for him nor his God, they decided to
play a trick on him. They would make a mock confession. So
they told the priest they did not care a straw for anything he
stood for and asked him for a suitable penance.

As the old man listened to them, as was his wont, he also listened to God. He took a pen and paper and he wrote, and handed them sealed the words he had written.

'This is your penance,' he said. 'Walk to the shrine outside the village. Open this note and read aloud what I have written.' Determined to carry the joke to its conclusion, the boys walked giggling and irresponsible to the shrine. And then in a loud voice they read:

> God made me – and I don't care a straw.
> God loves me – and I don't care a straw.
> Christ died for me – and I don't care a straw.

They lost their arrogant blasphemy and returned to find the mercy and lovingkindness of the Christ they had tried to mock.

## November 23rd

One of my favourite books is *Kristin Lavransdatter* written by Sigrid Undset (Nobel Literature Prizewinner) about her native Norway in the fourteenth century.

Kristin was burdened with a heavy sin, and despite the warmth and help of a wise priest, could not shed the burden. Finally he said to her, 'Kristin, dare you think in your wicked pride that sin of yours can be so great that God's lovingkindness is not greater?'

We must remember that God who is our Judge is also our Saviour and that we can if we surrender our sin 'bury it in the grave of our Redeemer'.

## November 24th

A more recent book which won the Whitbread Award is Christy Nolan's *The Eye of the Clock*. Joseph (who really represents Christy himself) had all the joy of winning the award, as a writer with cerebral palsy, only to have his joy shattered when he read a callous piece by an American writer who cast doubts on the authenticity of the work. He did not believe such a mind could dwell in such a body, even though Joseph had written a poem in his presence. Joseph could not get at the American critic, so, as we often do ourselves, he railed at God and at

Christ on the cross. How could God stand by and see a dumb disabled boy be attacked in such a way? Nobody knew of his rebellion, so nobody could help. He only found his peace by going back to the church where he had inwardly railed at God, and there he put things in perspective and was cleansed of his bitter feelings.

### November 25th
On General William Booth's entry into heaven:

> He saw King Jesus: they were face to face –
> He knelt a-weeping in that holy place.

### November 26th
What makes the desert beautiful is that somewhere, deep inside it, is a beautiful spring.
> *from* The Little Prince *by Antoine de Saint-Exupéry*

### November 27th
O LORD, I know that the way of man is not in himself: it is not in man that walketh to direct his steps. O LORD, correct me, but with judgment; not in thine anger, lest thou bring me to nothing.
> *Jeremiah 10:23–24 (AV)*

### November 28th
> I bind unto myself today
> The power of God to hold and lead,
> His eye to watch, his might to stay,
> His ear to hearken to my need.
> The wisdom of my God to teach,
> His hand to guide, his shield to ward,
> The word of God to give me speech,
> His heavenly host to be my guard.　　　*St Patrick*

**November 29th**

As this sometimes gloomy month is drawing to its close, I give
you a couple of poems which may raise a smile.

SAINT PETER

Saint Peter was a fisher, and
'Twas what he liked to be,
But still he didn't understand
His art like you or me.
He sunk his net – it's in the books –
And lifted fish in shoals,
He towed them in with mighty hooks
And roasted them on coals.

He's learnt a lot, I dare avow,
These nineteen hundred years,
No big sea-hooks for Peter now,
No hand-lines, nets or spears.
In gentle Walton he confides
(Our Isaak's learning too),
And hosts of Isaak's sons besides
Have told him what to do.

He kilts his coat (above, I think,
His apostolic knees),
Gives Andrew with a saintly wink
In charge the shining keys;
And speeds, light-hearted as a lad,
With reel and line and rod,
To float his fly where streams make glad
The City of our God.

*W. F. Marshall, the Bard of Tyrone*

## November 30th

THE IRISH PIG

'Twas an evening in November,
As I very well remember,
I was strolling down the street in drunken pride
But my knees were all a-flutter
So I landed in the gutter
And a pig came up and lay down by my side.

Yes, I lay there in the gutter
Thinking thoughts I could not utter
When a colleen passing by did softly say,
'Ye can tell a man that boozes
By the company he chooses.'
And with that the pig got up and walked away.

*Traditional*

# 'HOW FAR IS IT TO BETHLEHEM?'
## *Meditations as we approach Christmas*

### Approaching Christmas (1)

When our children were small, we had a visitor staying with us who was highly amused at their ingenuity when they were told it was bedtime. They produced the most amazing reasons for staying up. He told us the true story of Ruth in whose house he had previously been staying. Much to her consternation, she was put to bed when her parents were going out and she objected to just being left with a baby-sitter. Her mother listened to the loud protests for a while, and then quietly said, 'Ruth, I don't know what you're making all the fuss about. You know I've always told you that even if I'm not here, God is always with you.' That really put the tin lid on it. The child erupted in fury. 'I don't want God. I want somebody with skin on.'

I think that gives us a clue to what really happened that first Christmas.

> Veiled in flesh, the Godhead see
> Hail the Incarnate deity.

The older hymn-books use '*wrapped* in flesh' and perhaps that tells us more clearly that our God is to be found there – with skin on.

The loveliest name I think given to Jesus was the name Emmanuel, which means 'God with us'. We can sieve through all the historical facts; we can collect all the information of time, place and date; we can discard all the legendary details accumulated here and there. At the end we may well have a useful bit of argumentation and documentation. But it could all be colourless and arid if we have missed the central truth. Our human spirits cry out for more than a historical figure or an eternal idea or an abstract Creator. We want to find God in a person and know what he is like. That's why it is necessary to make a special journey each Christmas and in our hearts go back not only to Bethlehem but go again by a longer route – via Gethsemane and Calvary. A little baby throws out his arms in the crib at Bethlehem and we have a cameo of Calvary. The redemption of the world is wrapped in swaddling clothes.

> Though Christ a thousand times
> In Bethlehem be born,
> If he's not born in me
> My heart is all forlorn.

## Approaching Christmas (2)

Just because it is such a social occasion, we feel sometimes we are in danger of losing the true meaning of Christmas. Coping with all the ruthless commercialisation can make us feel that the birth in Bethlehem is just a cosy little happening 2000 years ago which is used to sell all the tinsel and the trappings and to try to gather up some goodwill here and there which has been lost throughout the year. The danger is in trivialising the occasion.

I have heard some hardened grown-ups scorn the Nativity plays which are performed all over the place at this time. I do not feel that they trivialise Christmas. For I feel I have seen some of the most wonderful expressions of joy and wonder, and even simple faith and trust, in these imperfect presentations of what took place that first Christmas. That has happened even on seeing Joseph enter, strangely knock-kneed, understandably looking like your village boy Peter. Or even when Mother Mary looks at the audience with that peculiar little squint, which you've only seen before when Joan, the ten-year-old from the village shop, came to school without her glasses. And what about the ad-libbing in the Crib scene? If you live in a tourist area as I do, you are quite likely to hear one helpful innkeeper tell Joseph to walk on and try the bed and breakfast place down the road.

In reality, Mary had travelled eighty rough miles that first Christmas, but it was also a journey of humility and suffering as well as adoration and joy. Mary had sung her Magnificat, which had in it the very stuff of revolution. He has filled those that are hungry. The rich he has sent empty away. He will cast down the mighty. He will exalt the humble. The blessedness which came to Mary was just the prelude to the sword which would pierce her heart thirty years on. Can we take the exquisite story as it is told in Luke's Gospel and possibly separate the prophecy from the history and the history from the symbolism? They are often so intermingled that it is just not possible to separate them. Perhaps we are not meant to, for every account is valuable in its own way. It can make some aspect of truth known. Indeed it will be the very essence of saving truth if it points us the way to Christ.

## Approaching Christmas (3)

If you had been in Bethlehem that first Christmas and asked why the crowds had travelled there and were milling about the city in such numbers, no one would have been able to tell you that the most important event in the history of mankind had come to pass. They would have no conception that ever after would be known as AD and all the time before as BC. They had merely travelled there to be counted as a number on a census. But to God each one was more than a number – each was a human being needing a Saviour. Let us not lose the importance of this great event for ourselves, for it's all too easy to find we are worshipping, not the incarnate Christ, but the tinsel on the Christmas tree.

### BC:AD

This was the moment when Before
Turned into After, and the future's
Uninvented timekeepers presented arms.

This was the moment when nothing
Happened. Only dull peace
Sprawled boringly over the earth.

This was the moment when even energetic Romans
Could find nothing better to do
Than counting heads in remote provinces.

And this was the moment
When a few farm workers and three
Members of an obscure Persian sect

Walked haphazard by starlight straight
Into the kingdom of heaven.                    *U. A. Fanthorpe*

## Approaching Christmas (4)

Christmas is a time for dreaming. We all give way to the child in us and do a bit of guessing as to what might be in that package hung on the tree and labelled with our name. Those who don't dream much at other times indulge their fancy when they wonder what Christmas morn will bring even though growing up means realising that to avoid over-expectation is the beginning of wisdom. Yet I believe we should dream. C. S. Lewis once said that because a child dreams of enchanted woods and trees that does not make him despise real woods. The real woods when he returned to them would be a little bit enchanted just because he had dreamt of fairy woods.

The months before that first Christmas were times of dreaming. Joseph and Mary had their visions; and great truths were revealed to them about a coming Saviour. Those were wonderful dreams, enchanted dreams, but the one which came to Joseph after the birth had less enchantment. It told them to prepare for a flight into Egypt for death was already threatening.

Our dreams are never better for us than what God wills for us. The shepherds who were coming off their night shift after caring for their flocks must have been fatigued and needing sleep. So they might well have thought they were having a dream or even a nightmare when the splendour of the Lord surrounded them. It does describe them as being terror-stricken. But they were reassured that it was all a reality and wonderful things were in store for them when they made their journey to the manger. I think it quite awe-inspiring that humble shepherds just completing their daily duties should be chosen as the first to declare to a wider company who the Christ Child was. The will of God for them was far better than their wildest dreams. In the frenetic activity and fatigue which accompanies us at this time, may we find time to dream a little.

> An azure sky, all star-bestrewn,
> A lowly crib, a hushed room,
> An open door, a hill afar,
> Where lambs and little shepherds are,
> To such a world, on such a night
> Came Jesus – little Lord of light.

## Approaching Christmas (5)

This is the story unearthed by Marco Polo in the late thirteenth century. During his travels throughout the world he searched for much obscure information, and part of his search was for the lost chronicles of the astrologer Sufi Abbas. After he had found the faded and tattered rolls of parchment for which he had been searching, he used to relate the story to his three daughters, and little by little the following myth took shape.

Gaspar, King of Tarshish, was black as ebony, young, tall, and handsome.

Balthazar, King of Ancient Chaldea, was middle-aged and of medium height and olive complexion.

Melchior, King of Nubia, was into old age, infirm, withered and shrunken in stature, pale as death.

They set out to follow the Star, to find this new King who had been foretold. On one point only they agreed – they were looking for someone noble, regal and wise. But each was expecting a King with the same skin as his own. At first they reasoned quietly about it, but as the journey progressed they became angry and contentious. The glory of the light of the Star they were following dimmed as they wrangled and disputed. Only when they became secretly ashamed of their warfare of words and sought again the early companionship they had enjoyed, did the Star shine brightly again.

Then they talked of what their secret aspirations were regarding their quest and where it would lead them. Gaspar the young and energetic monarch felt that, above all, the world needed a Sovereign Lord. He showed the gift that he had brought – the gift of gold for a truly royal personage.

Balthazar the middle-aged monarch felt that no earthly sovereign lord was sufficient. He longed for a revelation of God himself, and so he brought a gift of frankincense signifying worship. Melchior the old man, nearing as he knew the end of his life, dwelt on years past, with things left undone that he wished he had done, and things that he wished could be erased. What he was searching for was a Saviour. He instinctively knew that such a Saviour would also be a sufferer. So he took with him his gift of myrrh.

Eventually they arrived at Bethlehem only to be overcome

with chagrin and dismay, for the Star had led them to a baby cradled in a mother's arms as she sang. They all three listened.

'My soul doth magnify the Lord,' she sang.

'The LORD!' exclaimed Gaspar. 'Then I have found my Sovereign Lord.' And he offered his gift of gold.

Mary sang on. 'And my spirit hath rejoiced in God . . .'

'In GOD!' called out Balthazar. 'My search is ended.' And he gave his gift of frankincense to the Babe.

Mary's song continued. 'My soul doth magnify the Lord and my spirit hath rejoiced in God my Saviour.'

'My SAVIOUR,' echoed Melchior. And he presented his gift of myrrh.

So Gaspar found the Sovereign Lord for whom he had been searching. Balthazar recognised in Jesus the God whom he had been seeking, and Melchior met his Saviour who he realised could meet his deepest need.

> All Paradise
> Collected in one bud
> Doth sweetly rise
> From its fair virgin bed
> Omnipotence an infant's shape puts on
> Immensity becomes a little one.    *Joseph Beaumont*

## Approaching Christmas (6)

On Christmas Eve my mother read
The story once again
Of how the little child was born
And of the three Wise Men

And how by following the Star
They found Him where He lay
And brought Him gifts; and that is why
We keep our Christmas Day.

And when she read it all, I went
And looked across the snow,
And thought of Jesus coming
As He did so long ago.

I looked into the East and saw
A great star blazing bright;
There were three men upon the road
All black against the light.

I thought I heard the angels sing
Away upon the hill. . . .
I held my breath . . . it seemed as if
The whole great world were still.

It seemed to me the little Child
Was being born again . . .
And very near . . . and THEN somehow
Was NOW . . . or NOW was THEN.

*Edna Kingsley Wallace*

For unto us a child is born, unto us a son is given: and the government shall be upon his shoulder; and his name shall be called Wonderful, Counsellor, The mighty God, The everlasting Father, The Prince of Peace. *Isaiah 9:6 (AV)*

# DECEMBER

*At Christmas play and make good cheer*
*For Christmas comes but once a year.*

## December 1st

### A PILGRIM'S BLESSING

May the Babe of Bethlehem be yours to tend
May the Boy of Nazareth be yours for friend
May the Man of Galilee his healing send
May the Christ of Calvary his courage lend
May the Risen Christ his presence send
And his holy angels defend you to the end.

## December 2nd

How many observe Christ's birthday
How few his precepts.
Oh, 'tis easier to keep holidays
       than commandments.

*Benjamin Franklin*

## December 3rd

Some folk will already be hoping for a traditional white Christmas. Well, as someone has said, a snowdrift is a beautiful looking thing, unless it just happens to be blocking your driveway, or along the path you have to shovel, or blocking the road that leads to your destination.

## December 4th

### EX ORE INFANTIUM

Little Jesus, wast Thou shy
Once, and just so small as I?
And what did it feel like to be
Out of Heaven, and just like me?
Didst Thou sometimes think of *there*,
And ask where all the angels were?
I should think that I would cry
For my house all made of sky;

I would look about the air,
And wonder where my angels were;
And at waking 'twould distress me –
Not an angel there to dress me!
Hadst Thou ever any toys,
Like us little girls and boys?
And didst Thou play in Heaven with all
The angels that were not too tall,
With stars for marbles? Did the things
Play, *Can you see me?* through their wings? . . .
Didst Thou kneel at night to pray,
And didst Thou join Thy hands, this way?
And did they tire sometimes, being young,
And make the prayer seem very long?
And dost Thou like it best, that we
Should join our hands to pray to Thee?
I used to think, before I knew,
The prayer not said unless we do.
And did Thy Mother at the night
Kiss Thee, and fold the clothes in right?
And didst Thou feel quite good in bed,
Kissed, and sweet, and Thy prayers said?

Thou canst not have forgotten all
That it feels like to be small:
And Thou know'st I cannot pray
To Thee in my father's way –
When Thou wast so little, say,
Couldst Thou talk Thy Father's way? –

So, a little Child, come down
And hear a child's tongue like Thy own;
Take me by the hand and walk,
And listen to my baby-talk.
To Thy Father show my prayer
(He will look, Thou art so fair),
And say: 'O Father, I, Thy Son,
Bring the prayer of a little one.'

And He will smile, that children's tongue
Has not changed since Thou wast young!

*Francis Thompson*

## December 5th

Some of the ancient December customs have been transferred to the Christmas festival. In Scandinavia and Germany the holly is called Christ's thorn, perhaps because it bears its red berries in December.

John Donne said of Christ, 'He found a Golgotha, even in Bethlehem, for to his tenderness the straws were almost as sharp as the thorns after.'

Early Christians referred to holly as the righteous branch, and justified bringing it in to decorate God's house by the words from Isaiah 60:13: 'The glory of Lebanon shall come unto you, the fir tree, the pine tree and the box together, to beautify the place of my sanctuary.'

## December 6th

And in the sixth month the angel Gabriel was sent from God unto a city of Galilee, named Nazareth, to a virgin espoused to a man whose name was Joseph, of the house of David: and the virgin's name was Mary. And the angel came in unto her, and said, Hail thou that art highly favoured, the Lord is with thee: blessed art thou amongst women. And when she saw him she was troubled at his saying, and cast in her mind what manner of salutation this should be. And the angel said unto her, Fear not, Mary: for thou hast found favour with God. And behold thou shalt conceive in thy womb, and bring forth a son, and shalt call his name JESUS. He shall be great, and shall be called the Son of the Highest: and the Lord God shall give unto him the throne of his father David: and he shall reign over the house of Jacob for ever; and of his kingdom there shall be no end. Then said Mary unto the angel, How shall this be, seeing I know not a man? And the angel answered and said unto her, The Holy Ghost shall come upon thee, and the power of the Highest shall overshadow thee; therefore also that holy thing which shall be born of thee shall be called the Son of God.

*Luke 1:26–35 (AV)*

**December 7th**
Lord God,
You hide from us at all times a perfect knowledge.
Mystery and miracle surround us.
Where we do not fully understand, help us to trust,
And in trusting to go forward like Mary, ready to obey,
And in obeying to bring glory into the midst of our stricken world.

**December 8th**
Our family ran up against a tricky problem when all the children were very small. One of them asked Santa Claus for something it would be quite impossible to acquire. It was explained in very diplomatic terms that Santa Claus was not going to be able to fulfil the desire that year. We were all surprised at the philosophical sigh which greeted this news – followed by 'Oh well, I'll just have to ask Gentle Jesus then.'

And so we were all launched into all kinds of explanations so that the child's prayer would not 'come weeping back to him'. God was in a sense like Mum and Dad who occasionally said 'Yes', sometimes said 'No' and quite often said 'Wait!'

Little did we know how hard the road of prayer was going to be for us very soon to tread. Or how urgent were going to be our petitions. The one who had been so good at explaining to us such difficult matters fell ill, terminally ill. Was the answer to be 'Yes', 'No', or 'Wait!'?

> 'Twas he who taught us how to pray
> And he I know has answered prayer
> But it has been in such a way
> To almost drive us to despair.

We didn't keep the one we loved. But we did not abandon prayer. So what can we say? Nothing more than this: There has been no circumstance, however harrowing, where we could not testify, 'His grace has been sufficient.'

## December 9th

> Faith came singing into the room
> And the other guests took flight.
> Grief and anxiety, fear and gloom
> Fled out into the night.
> And I wondered that such peace could be,
> But Faith said gently, 'Don't you see
> They cannot live with me?'

## December 10th

The eternal stars shine out as soon as it is dark enough.   *Carlyle*

## December 11th

Interviewer to Evelyn Waugh: You have not much sympathy for the man in the street, have you, Mr Waugh?
Waugh: You must understand that the man in the street does not exist. He is a modern myth. There are individual men and women, each of whom has an individual and immortal soul, and such beings need to use streets from time to time.

## December 12th

The first forty years of life give us the text: the next thirty supply the commentary.   *Schopenhauer*

## December 13th

And Mary said, My soul doth magnify the Lord, and my spirit hath rejoiced in God my Saviour. For he hath regarded the low estate of his handmaiden: for, behold, from henceforth all generations shall call me blessed. For he that is mighty hath done for me great things; and holy is his name. And his mercy is on them that fear him from generation to generation. He hath shewed strength with his arm: he hath scattered the proud in the imagination of their hearts. He hath put down the mighty from their seats, and exalted them of low degree. He hath filled the hungry with good things; and the rich he hath sent empty away. He hath holpen his servant Israel, in remembrance of his mercy; as he spake to our fathers, to Abraham and his seed for ever.   *Luke 1:46–55 (AV)*

## December 14th

Look on us, O Lord,
and allow the darkness within our souls to disappear
    before the rays of your glory.
Fill us with your love and open up to us
    the treasures of your wisdom.
All that we wish for is known to you.
Come and bring to perfection, therefore,
what you have already begun,
    and what your Holy Spirit has guided us
    to ask of you in prayer.
We seek your face, Lord.
Show us your glory
    then all our longing will be satisfied
    and we shall know something
    of your perfect peace.
Through Jesus Christ our Lord.        *St Augustine (adapted)*

## December 15th

There is a lovely story often told at Christmas about three trees
which dreamt and talked together as they grew together on a
hillside. The first tree wished to be cut down and made into a
baby's cradle. The second wished to be made into a wonderful
ship carrying rich goods and precious jewels. The third didn't
particularly wish to be cut down, but just wanted to go on growing on the hillside, pointing its branches up to heaven. As time
passed the woodcutters came along, and the tree which had
wanted so much to be made into a cradle became a cattle stall.
And it was there that Jesus was born. The second one which
had wished to be a splendid ship was cut down and made into a
small fishing boat which was eventually lent to Jesus by Simon
Peter so that he could speak from it to the people on the shores
of Galilee. And the third which had just wanted to go on growing, had to be cut down because it was needed for a cross of
shame. But it was the Cross on which Christ the Saviour of the
world died – the same Christ who was the Babe in the cattle
stall; the same Christ who taught from Simon Peter's boat.

## December 16th

I have often wondered what it felt like to be Joseph, the humble carpenter of Nazareth, as he came to accept his part in the world-changing events that first Christmas. Here is part of an imagined scene from *Stable Talk* by Paul Burbridge and Murray Watts:

I made you a little bed. Proper little bed, all planed smooth with no nasty splinters. I set it on rockers and carved a little lamb on the headboard. You'll see it when we get back to Nazareth. You'll like it. Well, I hope so, because I wouldn't like you to think your father wanted you to be born in this old feeding trough. One of these legs is a bit wobbly. Well, that's nails you see. Never trust nails. That should have been jointed good and proper. Takes a little care, that's all. And now I've got to take care of you as well. I know who you are, you see. You don't know who I am, though, do you? I've not really had anything to do with you. I wish I was your father – you're so beautiful. But I'm just standing in, as you might say, for someone else. . . .

Do you know what I think? I think you are going to have your real Father's temperament. Because, you see, your Father is a loving, kind, mighty, glorious, everlasting God. And the angel in the dream told me you are going to save the people from their sins – which does seem a lot to ask of a little chap like you. But I think I shall be pretty proud of you anyway. You're still part of the family, you see. And it's a good family. Oh yes, we go back a long way. I may be only a carpenter, but your great, great, great, great, great grandfather was a King. There! He was King David. We've had kings, priests, farmers, carpenters and now we've got a king again.

## December 17th

The words a father speaks to his children in the privacy of his home are not overheard at the time, but, as in whispering galleries, they will be heard clearly at the end and in posterity.

*Richter*

## December 18th

JOSEPH

Who has not carolled Mary
And who her praise would dim?
But what of humble Joseph –
Is there no praise for him?

If Joseph had not driven
Straight nails through honest wood,
If Joseph had not cherished
His Mary as he should:

If Joseph had not proved him
A sire both kind and wise
Would he have drawn with favour
The Child's all-probing eyes?

Would Christ have prayed, 'Our Father'
Or cried that name on death,
Unless he first had honoured
Joseph of Nazareth?               *Gilbert Thomas*

## December 19th

Here all mankind is equal:
Rich and poor alike, they love their children.
                              *Euripides (480–406 BC)*

## December 20th

And it came to pass in those days, that there went out a decree from Caesar Augustus, that all the world should be taxed. (And this taxing was first made when Cyrenius was governor of Syria.) And all went to be taxed, every one into his own city. And Joseph also went up from Galilee, out of the city of Nazareth, into Judaea, unto the city of David, which is called Bethlehem; (because he was of the house and lineage of David:) to be taxed with Mary his espoused wife, being great with child. And so it was, that, while they were there, the days were accomplished that she should be delivered. And she brought forth her firstborn son, and wrapped him in swaddling clothes, and laid him in a manger; because there was no room for them in the inn.               *Luke 2:1–7 (AV)*

**December 21st**

Lord God, our Father in heaven, we thank you that you sent your Son to be a member of a human family, with all its varying emotions, activities, wills and temperaments. At this special and sometimes fraught period of the year, when there is so much busy-ness in our lives, help us to set aside time for you and for the many in our society who will not have any joy in family gatherings. We pray for the sick, the lonely, the homeless and all separated, either by their own desires, or by circumstances not of their making, from human fellowship and company. Be their and our close Companion. For the sake of your Son, our Redeemer.

**December 22nd**

Now for a little mirth.

CHRISTMAS PRESENTS

Have you ever noticed how grown-ups give each other
    presents?
There's no mystery and not a lot of fun.

Every year Grandma gets a tin of talcum powder.
She always says, 'Ah, my favourite!'
Even before she opens the wrapping.
Grandpa always says, 'Well, I know what's in here.
It's two pairs of socks. Just what I wanted!'

This year, Auntie Vi got an umbrella
    in an umbrella-shaped parcel.
I mean, it looks just like an umbrella.
And before Auntie Vi pulled the paper off,
She said to Mum, 'It will match that new coat of mine.'

As for Mum and Dad, they just sat there and said,
'We've given each other a joint present this year.
It's a digital clock radio for our bedroom.'
Do you know, they didn't even bother to wrap it
    up and put it under the tree!

At the end, when everything had been given out,
Mum said, 'We mustn't forget the gift-vouchers
    from Debbie and Jim.
We sent them a cheque for the same amount.'

We always do.'
I call that a bit unimaginative, don't you?

Maybe when you come to think of it
Grown-ups need Father Christmas far more
    than children do.                        *Roderick Hunt*

## December 23rd

In a school where I was teaching, a minister had been telling
the five-year-olds why Joseph and Mary had to journey to
Bethlehem. He talked about the census held in order to levy
taxes. He didn't seem to have much notion of the blissful ignorance of five-year-olds regarding the vexed question of taxes.
When the teacher asked the children later if they understood
why Mary and Joseph had had to go to Bethlehem, one little girl
answered brightly, 'They had to go to see about their cactus.'

## December 24th

### THE OXEN

Christmas Eve, and twelve of the clock,
    'Now they are all on their knees,'
An elder said as we sat in a flock
    By the embers in hearthside ease.

We pictured the meek mild creatures where
    They dwelt in their strawy pen,
Nor did it occur to one of us there
    To doubt they were kneeling then.

So fair a fancy few would weave
    In these years! Yet, I feel,
If someone said on Christmas Eve,
    'Come, see the oxen kneel

In the lonely barton by yonder coomb
    Our childhood used to know,'
I should go with him in the gloom,
    Hoping it might be so.          *Thomas Hardy*

**December 25th**

> Little man and God indeed
> Little and poor Thou art all we need.
> We will follow where Thou dost lead
> And we will heed
> Our brother Son of Mary.

**December 26th**

This is St Stephen's Day, more commonly known as Boxing Day. I wonder if the two names are connected, because Stephen was the first Christian martyr who died for his faith, and in the early years of Christianity he was one of seven deacons appointed to help look after the need of widows. Boxing Day was so-called as the day when the almsboxes were opened in the churches, and the money distributed by the priests to the needy.

**December 27th**

And when the days of her purification according to the law of Moses were accomplished, they brought him to Jerusalem, to present him to the Lord; (as it is written in the law of the Lord, Every male that openeth the womb shall be called holy to the Lord;) and to offer a sacrifice according to that which is said in the law of the Lord, A pair of turtle doves, or two young pigeons. . . . And Joseph and his mother marvelled at those things which were spoken of him. And Simeon blessed them, and said unto Mary his mother, Behold, this child is set for the fall and rising again of many in Israel; and for a sign which shall be spoken against; (Yea, a sword shall pierce through thy own soul also,) that the thoughts of many hearts may be revealed.                    *Luke 2:22–24, 33–35 (AV)*

**December 28th**

> Moonless darkness stands between,
> Past, O Past, no more be seen!
> But the Bethlehem star may lead me
> To the sight of Him who freed me
> From the self that I have been.
> Make me pure, Lord: Thou art holy;
> Make me meek, Lord: Thou wert lowly;
> Now beginning, and alway;
> Now begin, on Christmas day.
>
> *Gerard Manley Hopkins*

**December 29th**

If you're already wilting at the thought of all those thank-you letters to be written, take heart from the following poem:

### CHRISTMAS THANK-YOUS

> Dear Auntie
> Oh, what a nice jumper
> I've always adored powder blue
> and fancy you thinking of
> orange and pink
> for the stripes!
> How clever of you!
>
> Dear Uncle
> The soap is
> terrific
> So useful
> and such a kind thought
> and how did you guess that
> I'd just used the last
> of the soap that last Christmas brought?
>
> Dear Gran
> Many thanks for the hankies
> Now I really can't wait for the 'flu
> And the daisies embroidered
> in red round the 'M'
> for Michael
> how
> thoughtful of you!

Dear Cousin
What socks!
and the same sort you wear
so you must be the last word in style
and I'm certain you're right that the
luminous green
*will* make me stand out a mile.

Dear Sister
I quite understand your concern
it's a risk sending jam in the post
But I think I've pulled out
all the big bits
of glass
so it won't taste too sharp
spread on toast.

Dear Grandad
Don't fret
I'm delighted
So *don't* think your gift will
offend
I'm not at all hurt
that you gave up this year
and just sent me
a fiver
to spend.                                    *Mick Gowar*

## December 30th
Year's end is neither an end nor a beginning, but a going on, with all the wisdom that experience can instil in us. *Hal Borland*

## December 31st
And I said to the man who stood at the gate of the year: 'Give me a light that I may tread softly into the unknown.' And he replied: 'Go out into the darkness and put your hand into the hand of God. That shall be to you better than light and safer than a known way.'                    *M. Louise Haskins (1908)*

# FINIS

We shall not cease from exploration
And the end of all our exploring
Will be to arrive where we started
And know the place for the first time.    *T. S. Eliot*


May the road rise with you
And the wind be always
        at your back.
May the sun shine warm
        upon your face
The rain fall soft
        upon your fields
And until we meet again
May God hold you
        in the palm of his hand.

# INDEX OF PRAYERS

Other prayers have been composed by Elizabeth Urch.

# Acknowledgments

*I gratefully acknowledge permission to use copyright material. Thanks are recorded to those listed below. In some instances, despite my best endeavours I have been unable to find the source of some pieces or the executors of some authors. If any new information comes to light, redress will be made.*

**Betjeman, Sir John:** 'Diary of a Church Mouse': The late Sir John, and his executors and John Murray Publishers.

**Bonhoeffer, Dietrich:** 'Who Am I?' from *Letters and Papers from Prison*, 1971 edition, used by permission of SCM Press and Simon and Schuster.

**Bonze, Nachum:** 'Lord, Let Your Light Be Only For The Day': Thomas Yoseloff Ltd. London, publishers of *Golden Peacock Anthology of Yiddish Poetry*.

**Burbridge, Paul, and Watts, Murray:** Extract from 'Stable Talk', from *Red Letter Days*: Hodder and Stoughton and the Authors.

**Campbell, Joseph:** 'As a white candle': By permission of Simon Campbell, Co. Wicklow, Ireland: Copyright holder.

**Carter, Sydney:** 'Said Judas To Mary' and '34 to 17': Reproduced by permission of Stainer & Bell Ltd and Sydney Carter.

**Dale, Alan:** Rendering of Psalm 65 from *Winding Quest* by permission of Oxford University Press.

**Eliot, T. S.:** 'We shall not cease from exploration' from 'Little Gidding', *Four Quartets*, Faber and Faber Ltd.

**Fanthorpe, U. A.:** 'BC: AD': Peterloo Poets, 2 Kelly Gardens, Calstock, Cornwall PL18 9SA.

**Feiffer, Jules:** 'I used to be poor . . .': Jules Feiffer, New York.

**Fulghum, Robert:** 'All I Ever Needed To Know I Learnt In Kindergarten': Robert Fulghum, Seattle.

**Gibran, Kahlil:** From *The Prophet*, Alfred A. Knopf Inc., New York.

**Gowar, Mick:** 'Christmas Thank-Yous' from *Swings and Roundabouts*, HarperCollins.

**Hardy, Thomas:** 'The Oxen' by permission of Macmillan Press Ltd., Basingstoke.